Jonathan Edwards and the Stockbridge Mohican Indians

His Mission and Sermons

"God weaves together the golden threads of His love and truth in Christ with the dark threads of human sin and misery. This rich and informative study by Roy Paul traces those threads through the tapestry of Mohican history, especially as they intersect with the life of Jonathan Edwards. Edwards' sermons to the Mohicans, together with his advocacy for their often-abused rights, show us that God is not the God of one nation, but the God of all peoples. A fascinating read!"

Joel R. Beeke, President, Puritan Reformed Theological Seminary, Grand Rapids, MI

"For too long, the ministry of Jonathan Edwards to the Mohican Indians of Stockbridge has not received its due from historians. In this fascinating study, Roy Paul gives voice to traditional Mohican spirituality, captures the complicated political and relational situation in Stockbridge, and shows that Edwards' years at the mission were a time of fruitful missionary work rather than merely a time for authoring theological and philosophical treatises. The examination of Edwards' sermons in Stockbridge is a particularly helpful contribution. Both scholars and pastors will find Paul's book informative and, if they read it sympathetically, inspiring as well."

Nathan A. Finn, Provost and Dean of the University Faculty, North Greenville University, Tigerville, SC

"This is a fine introduction to Jonathan Edwards' ardent ministry to the Mahicans of Stockbridge, which is still the least understood aspect of his life. Especially valuable is Roy's presentation and analysis of Edwards' Stockbridge sermons, which have scared less courageous scholars away for many years. My prayer is that this book will both interest younger scholars in the study of Edwards' work during the 1750s and inspire faithful Christians to engage in humble, loving cross-cultural work today."

Douglas A. Sweeney, Author, *Jonathan Edwards and the Ministry of the Word: A Model of Faith and Thought*

"Roy Paul's work on the Mahican people and the mission at Stockbridge, Massachusetts, provides a new and vital perspective: beginning not with English missionizing, but with the Mahicans themselves. Their relation to Jonathan Edwards, highlighted here, is an important one, as illustrated through his sermons, but he is only a part of their story, a story of connection to place, of deep spirituality, and of survival and recovery."
Kenneth P. Minkema, Jonathan Edwards Center,
Yale University, New Haven, CT

"It has been my privilege to know Roy Paul, first as a fellow congregant, then as his pastor and, in recent years, as a fellow pilgrim committed to the study and teaching of Jesus the living Word, revealed in and through the written Word. From the outset I was struck by Roy's keen mind, which he has applied consistently over decades to the understanding, clarifying and proclamation of his faith and spirituality. However, unlike some academics, Roy brings a passionate heart to this effort. Hearing him describe the research that led to this book was all the assurance I needed to conclude that you will find herein the same confluence of reason and passion. You will also learn a lot about the Christocentric spirituality of Jonathan Edwards, America's foremost philosopher-theologian."
Sunder Krishnan, Pastor Emeritus, Rexdale Alliance Church,
Toronto, ON

"It has been a long while since I visited the New England awakening. I recall how I often sought the Lord for a similar moving in our own day. I rarely considered its impact on the native peoples. Roy Paul's research gives valuable insight to the way God prepared the Indian heart to receive the gospel. In spite of the failures of those associated with the Indian mission, the intrinsic beauty and sheer power of God's Word drew them irresistibly to the cross. This is an encouragement to every generation of believers who desire to be faithful in mission. Thank you for such a sweet blend of story, theology and devotion."
Bob MacGregor, Lead Pastor, Grandview Baptist Church,
Kitchener, ON

"The history of Europeans bringing Christianity to Native Americans is a complicated mess full of misunderstandings, mistakes, and—let's not mince words—murder. To undo the racist narrative of the valiant cowboy versus the savage Indian, educators have rewritten the historical narrative to portray Christians as the evil culprit behind the genocide. Sadly, this argument has some merit, but there is so much more to the story. With a passion for research and accuracy, Roy Paul strives to set the record straight about what happened when the first Christians of America interacted with their first neighbors. While there were men who used the religion of power for personal gain, there were also men who used the Gospel message of salvation to minister to the Natives. The most famous of these men was Jonathan Edwards, who ministered to my Mohican Nation and made a huge impact in their eternal lives as their earthly lives were coming undone."

Mark Shaw, Enrolled member of the Stockbridge-Munsee Band of Mohican Nation

"The Muh-he-con-neok have a rich and diverse history. From their homelands in the East to their current reservation in Wisconsin, they have never forgotten who they are and where they came from. Roy Paul has managed to combine the history of the Mohican people with the history of the tribes' Christianization in a way that is both respectful of their traditions and honest about the atrocities inflicted on them by colonization."

Heather Bruegl, M.A., Enrolled Oneida Nation of Wisconsin and Descendant Stockbridge Munsee; Director of Cultural Affairs-Stockbridge Munsee Community, Bowler, WI

"With the wealth of background knowledge of indigenous American peoples, Roy Paul unfolds an in-depth account of Jonathan Edwards' Stockbridge years and his preaching ministry there. Looking at Edwards as a 'missionary' has been an underdeveloped theme in the field. The textual expositions of primary sources dealing with Edwards' sermons to the Mohicans and Mohawks are particularly illuminating and make an important contribution to Edwards studies."

Chris Chun, Director of Jonathan Edwards Center and Professor of Church History, Gateway Seminary, Ontario, CA

ROY M. PAUL

JONATHAN EDWARDS AND THE STOCKBRIDGE MOHICAN INDIANS

HIS MISSION AND SERMONS

Foreword by MICHAEL A.G. HAYKIN

Jonathan Edwards and the Stockbridge Mohican Indians

Copyright © 2020 by Roy M. Paul

All rights reserved. This book or any portion thereof may not be reproduced or used in any manner whatsoever without the express written permission of the publisher except for the use of brief quotations in a book review.

Published by: H&E Publishing, Peterborough, Ontario, Canada
www.hesedandemet.com

Front cover image: The Treaty of Penn with the Indians, Benjamin West, 1771–1772
Back cover image: Edwards' portrait by Marco Rodrigues, 2019. Used with permission.

Many Trails symbol designed by tribal member Edwin Martin. Used with permission of the Stockbridge Munsee Band of Mohican Indians.

Paperback ISBN: 978-1-989174-53-1
Hardcover ISBN: 978-1-989174-57-9
eBook ISBN: 978-1-989174-54-8

A Chronology

5 October 1703	Jonathan Edwards born at East Windsor, Connecticut
1716-1720	Edwards attends Yale, Receives BA in 1720
1721	Edwards' conversion
1726	Begins apprenticeship to his grandfather, Solomon Stoddard, in Northampton, Massachusetts
15 February 1727	Edwards ordained at Northampton
28 July 1727	Edwards and Sarah Pierpont marry
11 February 1729	Stoddard dies. Edwards assumes the pulpit in Northampton
1734-1735	Revival in Northampton
13 October 1734	John Sergeant's first discourse to the Mohicans.
1737	Edwards publishes *A Faithful Narrative*
1738	Town of Stockbridge established
8 July 1741	Edwards Preaches *Sinners in the Hands of an Angry God* at Enfield, Connecticut
1746	Edwards publishes *Religious Affections*
9 October 1747	David Brainerd dies in Edwards' home
27 July 1749	John Sergeant dies
1748-1750	Controversy with his Northampton congregation
22 June 1750	Dismissed as pastor of the Northampton church
1 July 1750	Preaches farewell sermon to Northampton congregation
8 August 1751	Becomes pastor at Stockbridge, Massachusetts
December 1754	Publishes *Freedom of the Will*
16 February 1758	Assumes the presidency of College of New Jersey (Princeton)
23 February 1758	Inoculated for smallpox
22 March 1758	Death of Edwards
7 April 1758	Death of Esther Edwards Burr
2 October 1758	Death of Sarah (Pierpont) Edwards
1784	Mohicans move to New Stockbridge, New York
1818	Some Mohican families start for White River, Indiana. Before arrival land is transferred to the federal government. They return to New Stockbridge
1821	Land is procured from Menominee and Winnebago tribes along the Fox River in Wisconsin
1824-1825	Mohicans move to Bowler, Wisconsin
30 May 1830	Indian Removal Act signed by President Andrew Jackson
30 March 1883	Court of Indian Offenses established. Practice of Native religion declared illegal.
11 August 1978	American Indian Religious Freedom act signed by President Carter

Dedication

To the Mohican Indian tribal members.
A strong, brave and proud people.
I am honoured to call them "ndinnaukomawuuk"—my friends.

Contents

FOREWORD xv
  Michael A.G. Haykin

PREFACE xvii

1 A BRIEF HISTORY OF THE MOHICAN TRIBE 1
  Muh-he-ca-ne-ok—Their History 3
  Mission Beginnings 13
  The Mission to the Mohicans 16
  Establishment of Stockbridge 25
  The Mission Continues 33

2 MUH-HE-CA-NE-OK—THEIR SPIRITUALITY 41

3 THE STOCKBRIDGE BIBLE 55

4 JONATHAN EDWARDS 63
  Early Life and Education 64
  Edwards in Love and in Ministry 68
  Edwards Succeeds Stoddard 71
  Dismissal from the Northampton Pulpit 77
  Edwards in Stockbridge 87
  Edwards' Spirituality 102

5 SELECTIONS FROM THE SERMONS OF JONATHAN EDWARDS TO
THE STOCKBRIDGE MOHICAN INDIANS 123
  The First Sermon-January 1751 125
  Sermon to the Mohicans & Mohawks at the Treaty, August 16, 1751 . 135
  Sermon to the Stockbridge Indians-August, 1751 142
  Sermon to the Stockbridge Indians-March 5, 1755 153
  Sermon to the Stockbridge Indians-March, 1755 156
  Farewell sermon to the Stockbridge Indians-January 8, 1758 161
  Farewell sermon to the Stockbridge Indians-January 15, 1758 164

6 SUMMARY AND CONCLUSION 169

ACKNOWLEDGEMENTS 177
BIBLIOGRAPHY 179
SUBJECT INDEX 185
SCRIPTURE INDEX 191

FOREWORD

Michael A. G. Haykin

What prompted Jonathan Edwards to settle with his family in the small, out-of-the-way frontier village of Stockbridge, Massachusetts? Some have surmised that Edwards settled here because the rigours of ministry among a smaller congregation would prove minimal, and he could devote himself largely to his study and the major treatises that he wrote during his time in Stockbridge. In other words, some have viewed Edwards in Stockbridge almost like an academic scholar on an extended sabbatical. Samuel Hopkins, in the memoir of his mentor, seems to imply something like this when he states that God gave Edwards "a quiet retreat" at Stockbridge where he could pursue his writing. This view has been furthered by the belief that Edwards simply preached rehashed sermons from his Northampton years.

An initial clue as to why Edwards came to Stockbridge is found in the geographical location of the home in which Jonathan Edwards and his family lived during their sojourn in Stockbridge from 1751 to 1757. Though the house is long gone, its location is marked today by a sundial and it appears that Edwards purposely located it among the Mahican Indians of the town. In doing this he was making a clear statement, namely, that he had genuinely come to minister to these people. It is noteworthy in this regard that his son Jonathan Jr. would later recall that his boyhood friends were all Indians and that he never spoke English outside of the family circle. Edwards' large correspondence from this period of his life also reveals that his pre-eminent goal was to reach the Native Americans with the life-giving gospel. His sermons from this period show that the majority of them were not simply repeats of sermons that he had preached in Northampton, but brand-new sermons constructed with careful attention to the audience to whom they were to be preached and the end to which they were intended.

Edwards also had a great desire to see the world-wide advance of the kingdom of Christ, in which he was convinced that the conversion of the peoples of North America had a place. The life of David Brainerd and his work among the first peoples of America would have had an impact upon Edwards' thinking in this regard as he edited and published the life and diary of this eminent example of genuine evangelical spirituality. Edwards had thus maintained an interest in the success of the Stockbridge mission over the years and had persuaded his Northampton congregation to heavily invest in the work during the 1740s.

This focus of Edwards' Stockbridge years, though, has not been appreciated, clear evidence of which is the fact that up until 1999 not one of the sermons that he preached to the Stockbridge Indians had been published. A number of these sermons are now available in a volume of Edwards' sermons covering the years 1743 to 1758, volume 25 in the multi-volume critical edition of Edwards' works published by Yale University Press. They reveal Edwards as a missionary preacher who was able to communicate plainly and effectively in his new evangelistic sphere.

This work by Roy Paul is therefore very welcome as Dr. Paul details clearly and robustly not only Edwards' love for the Mahican Indians and his concerns for their eternal well-being, but also the larger historical context that led to this important ministry of Edwards among these First Peoples. As Dr. Paul demonstrates, Edwards' ministry had a significant legacy, not the least part of which is as an example to those today who are still vitally concerned for the expansion of the kingdom of Christ.

Michael A.G. Haykin, FRHistS
Dundas, Ontario
January 4, 2020

Preface

Were you to ask the average person in North America what they know about the Mohican[1] Indians their response would most likely be something like, "I have heard of the book *The Last of the Mohicans*, by James Fenimore Cooper." But anyone who has read this book or watched the movie adaptation of it and then ventured to learn more about the Mohican tribe and their history will quickly realize that there is little factual information about the Mohican people in this classic work. For a fictional story it is, with a little credible history blended with copious amounts of fiction to make it entertaining. The actual history of the Mohican people is much starker, however, and chronicles one of the darkest narratives in the history of the United States of America in its misdealing with the indigenous peoples of the land.

As will be demonstrated, the Mohicans were a people of faith, who believed that the Great Spirit was the provider and sustainer of all things. In their effort to find out more about the Great Spirit, they called upon the English, whom they believed were especially blessed by God, to teach them more about him. They trusted the missionaries sent to them, believing they spoke the truth and, indeed, many of the ministers fought diligently to ensure the Indians were treated fairly. Nevertheless, the wealthy, powerful, and corrupt government officials would always win out. The great "land grab" of the seventeenth and eighteenth centuries saw the various American Indian tribes systematically swindled out of their land holdings, only to be displaced to often worthless scrub properties. That is the true chronicle of the Mohican nation.

---

[1] Authors have used variant spellings such as Mohican and Mahican. They are interchangeable. This tribe is not to be confused with the Mohegans, who were part of the Peqout tribe. The present-day Mohegan reservation is located in Uncasville, Connecticut, while the Mohicans are located in Bowler, Wisconsin.

Here were a people once situated in the lush Delaware Valley of the eastern United States who today, those few that remain, reside on a reservation in remote Wisconsin.

This chronicle will begin with a history of the Mohican people and trace their movements up to the present. Here some key dates and events will be highlighted, along with prominent people who influenced the tribe and a summary of the current state of Christianity within the tribe. The following section will provide a biography of Jonathan Edwards, the second, and perhaps most influential Christian missionary, who came to the tribe in Stockbridge, Massachusetts in 1751, following the death of the first missionary, John Sergeant. Edwards would stay with the Mohicans, preaching to them each Sunday through an interpreter, until leaving in 1758 to assume the position as third President of Princeton University. Stockbridge was the first attempt to integrate English and Indian families into the same community, with the goal of teaching the Indians farming and animal husbandry skills and educating their young boys in boarding schools. Edwards preached twice on Sundays; once to the Mohicans through an interpreter, and once to the English settlers. To date, very few of Edwards' Indian sermons have been published.[2] To that end, the final section of this work will include an analysis of a number of sermons preached by Edwards to the Mohicans, with the goal of studying content, style and delivery.

---

[2] Wilson H. Kimnach, Kenneth P. Minkema and Douglas A. Sweeney, eds., *The Sermons of Jonathan Edwards, A Reader* (New Haven: Yale University Press, 1999), 105–110.

1
A Brief History of the Mohican Tribe

Anthropologists have long held that the indigenous peoples of North America originated in Asia, made their way across the Bering Strait when the land masses were joined between Russian and Alaska, and then slowly migrated southward over a period of about twelve millennia. Rutherford tells us:

> Until Columbus, the Americas were populated by pockets of tribal groups distributed up and down both north and south continents. There are dozens of individual cultures that have been identified by age, location, and specific technologies—and via newer ways of knowing the past, including genetics and linguistics. Scholars have hypothesized various patterns of migration from Beringia into the Americas. Over time, it has been suggested that there were multiple waves, or that a certain people with particular technologies spread from north all the way south.[1]

This very well may have been true of the Mohican tribe, for in writing their history, Capt. Hendrick Aupaumut (1757–1830), a Mohican chief, recorded that his people, "crossed the great water at the place

---

[1] Adam Rutherford, "A New History of the First Peoples in the Americas," *The Atlantic*, October 3, 2017, https://www.theatlantic.com/science/archive/2017/10/a-brief-history-of-everyone-who-ever-lived/537942/.

where this and the other country are nearly connected."[2] It is presumed that hardship and famine drove the people south in search of a better land to sustain them. Electa Jones, in writing the history of the Mohican people stated:

> A famine compelled them, "says the Muh-Hea-Ken-Neew History, to disperse themselves throughout the regions of the wilderness after sustenance—and at length lost their ways of former living, and apostatized. As they were coming from the West, they found many great waters, but none of them flowing and ebbing like Muh-he ku-nuk, until they came to Hudson River. Then they said to one another—this is like Muh-he-con-nuk, our nativity. And when they saw that game was very plenty in that country, they agreed to kindle fire there, and hang a kettle whereof they and their children after them may dip out their daily refreshment. (The name of the Hudson was Maliecanittuk.)[3]

Until 1609, when Henry Hudson sailed up the river that today bears his name, the Mohicans had lived in loosely knit communities, each with its own leader, in the Delaware Valley along the river. Hudson had been commissioned by the Dutch East India Company to search out an eastern route to Asia, however, finding his northerly route around Norway blocked by ice, he turned his ships westward, ultimately landing in Newfoundland. He continued his explorations of the Atlantic coast and eventually up the river. His explorations would forever change the lives of the Muh-he-ka-ne-ok: "People of the Waters That are Never Still."[4]

---

[2] Electa F. Jones, *Stockbridge Past and Present, or, Records of an Old Mission Station* (Springfield, MA: Samuel Bowles & Company, 1854), 2–3.

[3] Jones, *Stockbridge*, 3.

[4] *A Brief History of the Mohican Nation Stockbridge-Munsee Band* (Bowler, WI: Stockbridge-Munsee Historical Committee, 2017), 3.

Muh-he-ca-ne-ok-Their History[5]

"How, then, can they call on the one they have not believed in? And how can they believe in the one of whom they have not heard? And how can they hear without someone preaching to them?" (Rom. 10:14).[6]

When Hudson returned to Europe from his voyage and presented the furs he had obtained from the indigenous peoples, the Dutch were quick to lay claim to the new land and sent a number of expeditions back to America. Marco Ramerini notes:

> In 1614 the Staten Generaal of the United Provinces of the Netherlands granted a charter for three years to the New Netherlands Company of Amsterdam. The first Dutch settlement in North America was built in late 1614 on Castle Island (an island in the Hudson River just South of Albany, NY). This trading post was called Fort Nassau, but this fort frequently lay under water and was consequently abandoned in 1617. In 1621, the newly founded West Indische Compagnie (WIC) was granted a charter, which included the coast and countries of Africa from the Tropic of Cancer to the Cape of Good Hope and also all the coast of America.[7]

During this time the Dutch were at war with England and on September 8, 1664, the British took possession of New York. While the Dutch retook the land in 1673, the Treaty of Westminster, signed in February

---

[5] For the purposes of this work only a brief history of the Mohicans is given, with key dates and events. Many scholars have recorded a more complete story of the tribe. See Jones, *Stockbridge*; Patrick Frazier, *The Mohicans of Stockbridge* (Lincoln: University of Nebraska Press, 1992); Rachel Wheeler, *To Live Upon Hope* (Ithaca, New York: Cornell University Press, 2008); Jeffrey Siemers, *Proud and Determined: A History of the Stockbridge Mohicans, 1734-2014* (Fond du Lac, Wisconsin: Big Smokey Press, 2013), and Samuel Hopkins, *Historical Memoirs, Relating to the Housatunnuk Indians* (Boston: S. Kneeland, 1753).

[6] All Scripture references are from the NIV unless otherwise stated.

[7] Marco Ramerini, "Dutch New York: The Dutch settlements in North America," Colonial Voyage, https://www.colonialvoyage.com/dutch-new-york/ (accessed July 25, 2019).

1674, saw it given back to the English. Part of the treaty conditions ensured continued trade and commerce for the Dutch merchants from America.

The Delaware Valley was lush and held an abundance of wildlife; a perfect setting for sustaining the needs of the indigenous tribes who lived there as peaceful hunter/gatherers; for even then the native peoples were committed to practicing a conservationist lifestyle. Aupaumut recorded of his people,

> They were not to kill more than necessary, for there was none to barter with them that would have tempted them to waste their animals, as they did after the Chuh-ko-thuk [white men] came on this Island; consequently, game was never diminished.[8]

However, their quiet, and for the most part peaceful lives, only interrupted by the occasional conflict with neighboring tribes, were about to be disrupted and forever changed. The European settlers that were to descend upon them were predominantly from two different streams—those fleeing religious persecution from rulers supporting Roman Catholicism; and shrewd entrepreneurial businessmen, looking to become wealthy from the abundance found in the New World. Subsequently, the European traders set up trading posts where the Indians could bring highly prized beaver pelts and deer skins and exchange them for a new form of weapon, the musket, as well as for warmer clothing items. Besides the social and financial devastation the natives would endure from dealing with the traders, their physical numbers would also be dramatically depleted, as the Europeans brought deadly communicable diseases such as small pox and tuberculosis, and the deadliest poison of all—alcohol.

While it is possible that the traders first traded alcohol with the natives out of ignorance, they soon realized the power it had over them,

---

[8] Bernd C. Peyer, ed., *American Indian Nonfiction: An Anthology of Writings, 1760s–1930s* (Norman: University of Oklahoma Press, 2017), 64.

and quickly used it to their trading advantage. Alcohol would not only destroy the Indians' physical bodies, but also their mental and spiritual constitution, rendering them pliable to the conniving traders and removing their ability to lead the productive lives they had previously enjoyed. Perhaps it is ironic that the native peoples introduced tobacco to the Europeans, which over the centuries has also proved to be detrimental to their own physical health and well-being.

Early on, the Mohicans realized the detrimental effect of alcohol on their people and pleaded with the authorities to legislate its sale to the Indians. In 1722, Mohican Chief Aupaumut wrote to the Governor of New York:

> When our people come from hunting to the town or plantations and acquaint the traders and people that we want powder and shot and clothing, they first give us a large cup of rum. And after we get the taste of it crave for more so that ... all the beaver and peltry we have hunted goes for drink, and we are left destitute either of clothing or ammunition. Therefore we desire our father to order the tap ... to be shut and to prohibit ... selling of rum, for as long as the Christians will sell rum, our people will drink it.[9]

The traders also introduced the Indians to firearms, which meant the Mohicans could hunt more quickly and efficiently than they had with spears and bows. Ultimately, this development led to depletion of the wildlife near the Hudson River, which necessitated the tribes' move east in search of more animals; for not only was wildlife a valuable trade item, but it was also their main source of sustenance. So began the first of many displacements for the River Indians, as they were then known.

Subsequently, they moved and resettled in the Housatonic Valley, near the Housatonic River. Frazier concurs:

---

[9] Quoted in Frazier, *The Mohicans*, 7.

The Mohicans depended on deer for food and clothing as a medium of exchange. Without it or some other barter item they would incur debts that often led to trouble. Some were perceptive enough to see that one of the causes of their dependent and weakened state since the Europeans' arrival was the use of animals as a commodity rather than as a staple. Konkapot [a Mohican chief] and his fellow tribesmen had once lived closer to the Hudson, but moved east to the Housatonic, where among other things it was less crowded and where game was probably more plentiful.[10]

While not the first effort to take over the Mohicans' land, the treaty of April 25, 1724 was to be a key event for the tribe in that it brought together the principal leaders who would ultimately figure in the establishment of Stockbridge, Massachusetts—the first integrated village of English settlers and Indians—in 1735. Until this time the Mohicans had lived in small communities along the river, each with its own Sachem, or Chief. Two of the major settlements were Wnahktukook, whose chief was called Konkapot and Skatehook, whose chief was Umpachenee. Because their tools were crude and rudimentary, the crops the River Indians could cultivate were limited to "Indian corn, beans, and little squashes."[11] The farm work was done by the women, young boys, and elderly men who were no longer able to go out hunting. The men were not only the hunters, but also sat in council to discuss issues related to their families and the tribe as a group. Their weapons for hunting were the bow and snares. While some small game was hunted all year, the larger hunt, to supply their ongoing needs, was divided into two seasons. Tribal Chief and historian Hendrick Aupaumut recorded:

> They hunted occasionally whole year; but hunting seasons are properly divided into two parts of a year. In fall they hunt for dear, bear, beaver, otter, raccoon, fisher, martin, for their

---

[10] Frazier, *The Mohicans*, 11.
[11] Peyer, *American Indian Nonfiction*, 64.

clothing, and drying meat for the ensuing season; and in the beginning of March they used to go out to hunt for moose on the Green Mountains, where these animals keep for winter quarters. From thence they go again for beaver hunting as soon as the rivers, ponds and creeks are opened ...[12]

Additionally, the fresh water of the Housatonic River provided an abundance of fish. In the spring of each year they would venture into the forest to gather the fresh maple sap and boil it down to syrup or make sugar. The Mohican people not only enjoyed the abundance of the land and water, but also good health, before the Europeans brought disease. "And as our ancestors were not subject to so many disorders, or sicknesses, as they were after the Chuk-ko-thuk, or white people settled amongst them, they flourished in some measure—that before they began to decay."[13] Aupaumut boasts that when called upon to go to battle, they could readily field one thousand warriors. Sadly, today that number has been reduced to approximately 1500 enrolled tribal members, with about 800 of them living on or near the reservation in Wisconsin.[14] Frazier states:

> While the Mohicans' own population had decreased probably tenfold, the Hudson River Valley population was increasing as rich descendants of the Dutch patroons multiplied and installed tenants on their extensive domains, many of which had been obtained from the Mohicans legally or illegally. From the east and the south the Mohicans were being pressed by expanding New England populations moving from the rich and entrepreneurial Connecticut River Valley.[15]

---

[12] Peyer, *American Indian Nonfiction*, 64.
[13] Peyer, *American Indian Nonfiction*, 64.
[14] *A Brief History*, 7.
[15] Frazier, *The Mohicans*, xii.

The English in the Connecticut River Valley were very well settled and becoming quite successful and influential. One of the most important and powerful families were the Stoddards of Northampton. The patriarch, Solomon Stoddard (1643–1729) was a preacher of great impact, and under his ministry there had been a number of revivals. Around 1723, Stoddard preached a sermon entitled, "QUESTION Whether GOD is not Angry with the Country for doing so little towards the Conversion of the *Indians?*" In his homily, Stoddard speculated, "That GOD is [angry] with the Country, and has been these threescore years, has been evident by His sending *Epidemical Discases* [sic] *and Devourers.*"[16] He stated that even though the Indians clearly demonstrated that they were aware of God and professed that it was he who was the great creator, this did not excuse Christians from preaching the gospel to them. He cites the Great Commission from Matthew 28:19 and says, "Hence it is evident, That it is the Mind of Christ, that Christian People as they have Opportunity, do in all generations, Labour to Christianize the Heathen."[17] Stoddard goes on to chide his hearers, reminding them that it was part of a Royal decree that they preach to the Indians but that many of them were too busy taking advantage of the poor souls. For that, God was rightly punishing them. He states:

> The Profession of those that Adventured into this Country was, that it was their principal design, to bring the Indians to the knowledge of the true God and Saviour of Mankind, and the Christian Faith; as the King declares in the Charter: The like is expressed in the Charter for Connections. And it would have been the Honour of the Country, if they had answered that Profession. Indeed we gave the Heathen an Example;

---

[16] Solomon Stoddard, "Question whether God is not Angry with the Country for doing so little towards the Conversion of the Indians?" Evans Early American Imprint Collection, https://quod.lib.umich.edu/cgi/t/text/text-idx?c=evans;cc=evans;view=text;idno=N02091.0001.001;rgn=div1;node=N02091.0001.001:1. (accessed June 25, 2019). Italics in original.

[17] Stoddard, "Question," 7.

and if they had not been miserably besotted, they would have taken more notice of it. But we have done very little to Answer our Profession. Some few pious persons, of their own accord, have taken some Pains, and had some Success. And some Money that has been contributed in England for the furtherance of that Design, has been faithfully expended that way: But the Country has been at very little Cost for the Conversion of the Heathen. Many Men have been more careful to make a booty of them, than to gain them to the practice of Religion. It puts me to a stand to conjure what Excuse can be made for this Neglect. The Poverty of the Country will be no Apology for this Omission. We have great cause to be humbled, that we have answered our profession so poorly.[18]

Wheeler notes, "But it was not only from pulpits that the Stoddard clan wielded influence. Members of the prominent family ruled—with the nearly unanimous support of the people—virtually every realm of life in western New England, from the religious to the civil to the military."[19] Solomon's son, John Stoddard was not only a devout Christian, but a highly successful and significant figure in the Connecticut Valley, and his career had covered every major sphere of public influence. In 1704, John had been a lieutenant in the militia stationed at Deerfield, during Queen Anne's War. When a detachment of French and Indians from Canada attacked Deerfield on February 29, Stoddard was at the home of his brother-in-law, Rev. John Williams. When the attack was over, forty-seven villagers were dead and one hundred twelve were taken captive to Canada. Stoddard alone survived in the Williams home, while others were taken captive. Wheeler recounts,

> Several of Stoddard's relatives would eventually be returned from their captivity in Canada, including John Williams and his sons Samuel and Stephen. Stoddard's niece, Eunice, however, would remain throughout her life the unredeemed

---

[18] Stoddard, "Question," 9–10. Italics in original.
[19] Wheeler, *To Live*, 19.

captive, committing the double betrayal of becoming a Catholic and living as an Indian, married to a Mohawk man at the Catholic-Mohawk community at Caughmawagha.[20]

Being acutely aware of the volatility of the political situation and the unpredictability under which New Englanders were living, Stoddard devoted his life to ensure a measure of safety and stability within his sphere of influence. Wheeler tells us,

> Securing his first government office in 1703 as registrar of probate, Stoddard would accumulate a handful of titles and offices over the coming decades, as justice of the peace, judge of the informal court of common pleas, colonel of the northern regiment of the Hampshire militia and member of the Massachusetts House of Representatives.[21]

Since New England settlers were eager to secure property along the fertile Housatonic River, and because the residents of Northampton had previously been successful in obtaining land from the River Indians, in 1722 Governor Jonathan Belcher called on John Stoddard to negotiate with the Mohicans to procure property in the area of what would become the first integrated community of whites and Indians—Stockbridge, Massachusetts. It is possible that Stoddard was already known to the Indians, which would have aided in the negotiations. Stoddard's efforts proved successful and on April 25, 1724, the Housatonic lands were purchased for the sum of four hundred sixty pounds, three barrels of cider and thirty quarts of rum. The deed, in part, reads:

> Know all men by these presents that we, Conkepot, Poneyote, Partarwake, Naurnauquin, Waenenocow, Nawnausquan, Cauconaughfeet, Nonamcaumet, Naunhamiss, Sunkhunk, Popaqua, Taunkhonkpus, Tartakim, Sauncokehe,

---

[20] Wheeler, *To Live*, 19.
[21] Wheeler, *To Live*, 21.

Cancannap, Sunkiewe, Nauheag, Mauchewaufeet, John VanGilder, Pinaskenet, all of Housatonack allias Westonook in New England, in ye province of ye Massachusetts Bay: for & in consideration of a valuable sum well secured by bond viz Four Hundred and Sixty Pounds, Three Barrels of Sider & thirty quarts Rum: bearing date with these Presents, under ye hand and seal of Capt. John Ashley of Westfield in ye County of Hampshire; we have given, granted, bargained, sold, aliened, conveyed, & confirmed, and doe by these presents, fully, clearly and absolutely give, grant, bargain, sell, allinate, convey & confirm unto Col. John Stoddard, Capt. John Ashley, Capt. Henry Dwight & Capt. Luke Hitchcock Esqrs, all in the County of Hampshire, Committee appointed by ye General Court to purchase a certain Tract of land lying upon Housatonack River, allias Westonook, in order for the settling two towns there ... we the aforesaid Indians have herunto set our hands and seals this 25th day of April, in ye tenth year of his Majisty's rign [sic] and in ye year of or[our Lord] one thousand seven hundred & twenty four ...[22]

Except for the disproportionate use of alcohol in the sale agreement, it is hard to place a current value on what the four hundred fifty pounds would have meant to the River Indians. What is very clear from reading the document is that the deed is phrased in "legalese." Very few of the Mohican people spoke fluent English, let alone would have understood the terms and conditions to which they were agreeing. So why would the Mohicans readily wish to part with their claim to the lands along the Housatonic? It was likely the case that resources were being depleted and the resulting difficulty in obtaining sufficient furs and trade goods to exchange for the highly desired European products, such as muskets and ammunition, forced them to use the only thing of value left to them in exchange—their land.[23]

---

[22] Harry Andrews Wright, ed., *Indian Deeds of Hampden County* (Springfield MA: 1905), 116–119.

[23] Shirley W. Dunn, *The Mohican World: 1680-1750* (Fleischmanns, NY: Purple Mountain Press Ltd., 2000), 70–75.

From this point forward, there were two principal Mohican chiefs who would figure greatly in interactions with the English settlers. They were Konkapot, one of the signatories on the land transfer deed of 1724, chief in Wnahktukook and Umpachenee, the chief in Skatehook. These two chiefs had previously served the English faithfully in a military capacity and were given commissions by Governor Jonathan Belcher; Umpachenee became a Lieutenant and Konkapot, a Captain. Little is definitively known about Umpachenee, and what can be pieced together comes from several scant references to him; a number of them from Moravian records. His Mohican name was Umpachenee, or Sonkenewenaukheek, however he was better known to the English as Aaron, or Lieutenant. He was married to the daughter of the Mohican "King" Etowaukaum, who had been part of a party of four senior Indian leaders who had travelled to England in 1710 to meet with Queen Anne. It may well have served as a strategic marriage, as it enabled them to bring two groups of Indians together. Wheeler states, "The marriage likely cemented an important alliance between Hudson River Mohicans and Housatonic peoples."[24] But there was another issue that weighed heavily on the hearts of these four Indian "kings" and another purpose that brought them before the Queen: "One of the goals of the Indians' visit was to request that English missionaries be sent to instruct the Indians in the Christian religion. Etowaukaum's willingness to ask the Queen for a missionary signaled his interest in Christianity for the Indians."[25]

More details are known of Konkapot. Besides being referred to as "Captain," he also took on the name John. Samuel Hopkins (1721–1803), in recounting the history of the Mohicans in his memoirs, written in 1753, says,

> Konkapot, the principal Person among them, was soon taken Notice of by the *English*, and spoken of as a Man of Worth. It

---

[24] Wheeler, *To Live*, 21.
[25] Dunn, *The Mohican World*, 161.

was by a mere Accident I became acquainted with his general character. Mr. *Ebenezer Miller*, one of my neighbours, who had his Account from *Housatunnuk*, inform'd me that he was strictly temperate, a very just and upright Man in his Dealings, a Man of Prudence, and industrious in his Business; and inclined to embrace the Christian Religion. [26]

Mission Beginnings

Hopkins, like Stoddard, was among a group of people who saw their responsibility as the evangelization and civilization of the River Indians, and met with Stoddard at his home on March 11, 1734. Stoddard's feeling was that if a mission to the Indians was to meet with any success, the missionary would have to reside with them. He cites as an example three men—Parker, Hinsdel and Secomb—and how their missionary efforts were limited to when the Indians came to the forts and outposts to trade and were probably not in the best state of mind for evangelism. This would have been especially true had the Indians been plied with rum during the trading transactions. Stoddard states that those Indians had also been under the influence of the French, probably indicating that much of the evangelization was Roman Catholic. This seemed to be the general consensus among the New England clergy, for Rev. Benjamin Colman, in a letter to William Grant on December 25, 1733 said, "Yet Clouds and darkness do very much encompass this excellent attempt more especially from ye prejudices of Popery sewn in ye minds of ye Salvages [*sic*] by ye French Jesuits and Friars."[27] All told, their exposure to the gospel would have been brief, and not under the best of conditions. Ultimately, all three men abandoned the missionary effort.

However, Stoddard thought there might be a better strategy when it came to evangelizing the Housatonic tribe. "But as to the *River Indians*, ... A *Missionary* might live among them, and take all Opportunities to instruct, not only the Men, but also their Families: their Children

---

[26] Hopkins, *Historical Memoirs*, 2. Italics in original of all Hopkins' references unless otherwise stated.

[27] Quoted in Wheeler, *To Live*, 32.

might be taught to read, and write, and be led into Knowledge of the Principles of Christianity, &c., &c."[28] This discussion encouraged Hopkins and he contacted the Rev. Stephen Williams, who was one of the sons of Rev. John Williams of Deerfield that had been taken captive, along with his family, during the massacre in 1704. Despite what he had experienced, he had a strong compassion for the Indians and longed to see the gospel brought to them. A letter was sent to the Commissioners in Boston and, when the response was very favorable, they requested that Samuel Hopkins and Stephen Williams be sent to the Indians of the Housatonic. On November 22, 1735, Governor Jonathan Belcher addressed the Government with the following plea:

> Gentlemen, ... I have lately received letters from several of the worthy Members of the Honourable Corporation in *England* for Propagating the Gospel among the Original Natives of this Country, signifying the good Disposition of that Honourable Company still to extend and increase that excellent Charity to the Souls of the poor Heathen: And since this Government has done so little from the first Settlement of the Country to this Day for the Conversion of the Indian Natives to the true Christian faith, altho' it is declar'd in the Royal Charter to have been the Principal end of our Ancestors in Settling this Plantation: I heartily wish the Assemble wou'd now encourage the spreading of the Gospel of Jesus Christ, among the Indians, on such conditions as may be agreed on between a Committee of this Court, and the Commissioners here of the said Corporation, and this wou'd also be one good means of civilizing the Indians, and of better cementing our Friendship with them.[29]

The timing of these events was providential, for early in 1734 there was an indication that the Housatonic Indians were open to hearing a proposal on the establishment of a mission among them. In May, Konkapot

---

[28] Hopkins, *Historical Memoirs*, 3.
[29] *Journals of the House of Representatives of Massachusetts*, v.12, 1734–1735 (Boston: Massachusetts Historical Society, 1919–1990), 94–95.

and Umpachenee travelled to Springfield to meet with Governor Belcher and receive the military commissions bestowed on them. Williams and Hopkins took the opportunity to meet with them to discuss bringing to the Housatonics a missionary who would enlighten them as to the Christian faith, and to educated them in English and agriculture. Their response to the proposal was lukewarm but they were willing to give it some consideration. Konkapot, it seems, had some inclinations towards Christianity, but also some serious misgivings. Not only was he concerned that if he were to embrace Christianity, he would be "discarded" by his people, he was also troubled by the speech and actions of the professing Christians he had come into contact with—who were as bad and sometimes worse than "the Heathen."[30] Of the two, Frazier tell us Umpachenee was the more skeptical. "Umpachenee was less enthusiastic about the proposal but said that he would not stand in the way of a mission. Though skeptical, less temperate, and prouder than Konkapot, he had compassion for his people and knew that the old beliefs did not serve them. Umpachenee had considerable influence among the Housatonics, so his opinions carried weight."[31] The Indian leaders told Hopkins and Williams that they could only speak for themselves and that the proposition would have to be heard and approved by the tribal council. They all agreed to a joint meeting to be held in July of that year.

When it came time for the meeting on July 9th, Rev. Hopkins was ill, so Stephen Williams was joined by Rev. Nehemiah Bull, from Westfield. Hopkins recorded,

> The *Captain* and *Lieutenant* were very glad to see them, and call'd their People together, of whom those Gentlemen inquir'd, whether they were willing a *Minister* be sent to them to instruct them in the *Christian Religion*, to teach their Children to read, &c.[32]

---

[30] Hopkins, *Historical Memoirs*, 2.
[31] Frazier, *The Mohicans*, 17.
[32] Hopkins, *Historical Memoirs*, 4. Italics in original.

After the presentations were made, the tribesmen deliberated for four days. Rev. Williams later reported that the discussions were too tedious to document, however he was particularly struck with a comment made by one Indian named Ebenezer Poohpoonuc:

> The Indians (says he) still continue in their Heathenism, notwithstanding the Gospel has been bro't so near them, and they are greatly diminished; so that since my remembrance, there were Ten Indians, where there is now One: But the Christians greatly increase and multiply, and spread over the Land; let us therefore leave our former courses and become Christians.[33]

The deliberations were successful and the Indians agreed to have a Missionary come to them. Hopkins records that "at the End of those Days they all gave in their Names, and signify'd their Desires to those Reverend Gentlemen, that a *Minister* might be sent to them, for the Ends propos'd."[34]

The Mission to the Mohicans

Subsequent to their acceptance by the Indians, Williams and Bull reported back to the Commissioners in Boston. The Commissioners were encouraged by the report and mandated that Williams and Bull search out a suitable person "to instruct them and their Children in Religion and in Reading, and to preach the Gospel to them on the Sabbaths."[35] As a salary, they designated the sum of £100 per annum "for his Encouragement."

---

[33] "Gospel ministers must be fit for the Master's use, and prepared to every good work, if they would be vessels unto honour: illustrated in a sermon preached at Deerfield, August 31. 1735. At the ordination of Mr. John Sargent, to the evangelical ministry, with a special reference to the Indians of Houssatonnoc, who have lately manifested their desires to receive the Gospel," (Boston: S. Kneeland & T. Green, 1735), iv.

[34] Hopkins, *Historical Memoirs*, 4.

[35] Hopkins, *Historical Memoirs*, 5.

As it was, Williams and Bull were aware of a young man, John Sergeant (1710–1749), who at the time was a tutor at Yale. He had once remarked "that he had rather be employ'd as a *Missionary* to the *Natives*, if a Door should open for it, than accept a call any *English* Parish might give him."[36] In September of 1734, they made an offer to him on behalf of the Commissioners. Fortunately, Sergeant kept a diary, and we hear, in part, his own response:

> I told the Gentlemen, that I was so far from being unwilling to devote myself to the Service of God in so good a Cause, that I was rather desirous, if none better qualify'd could be found, to improve what Abilities I had in such an Undertaking; tho' I was sensible, I must not only lose a great many agreable [*sic*] Amusements of Life, especially in leaving my Business at *College*, which was the most agreable to me that could be; but also expose myself to many Fatigues and Hardships, and I know not to what Dangers, among a barbarous People. For indeed I should be asham'd to own myself a *Christian*, or even a *Man*, and yet utterly refuse doing what lay in my Power, to cultivate Humanity among a People naturally indigenous enough, but for Want of Instruction, living so much below the Dignity of Human Nature; and to promote the *Salvation* of *Souls perishing in the Dark*, when the *Light of Life* is so near them.[37]

Sergeant's view of the Housatonics as "barbarous" and lacking human dignity is a clear demonstration of how ignorant most Europeans were in regard to the Indians. As was to be demonstrated in the ensuing years, it was the treatment of the Indians by the English that would be barbarous and lacking any sense of fairness and dignity. Sergeant's motivation to bring them the gospel was from a noble heart, however, and he goes on in his diary to state that a further reason for evangelizing the

---

[36] Hopkins, *Historical Memoirs*, 5.
[37] Hopkins, *Historical Memoirs*, 6.

Indians was so that they would grasp the true gospel and not be corrupted by the Roman Catholics, who were making inroads in America. Sergeant said, "Besides to see so much Pains taken by those of the *Romish* Church, not only in other Parts, but also in *America*, and in our Borders, whose Religion is so corrupted, that it may scarcely be call'd Christianity."[38]

On October 8, 1734 Sergeant went to Nehemiah Bull's and on the 11th the men set out to meet up with the Indians. They planned to stay overnight at the only house on the way, but when darkness overtook them, they spent the night, without shelter, in the woods. They got to the Indians the next day and on the 13th of October, Sergeant gave his first discourse to the Mohicans. The interpreter was Ebenezer Poohpoonuc, whose English was quite good. Though Poohpoonuc had been previously instructed in Christianity, he had not been committed to it; after hearing Sergeant, however, he voiced his desire to be baptized. The usual Calvinist practice of the time was to ensure a believer was catechized before being baptized. However, the next day, as Rev. Bull examined him in his understanding of the Christian faith at the home of Lieut. Umpachenee, Bull and Sergeant were satisfied that he was well versed in his faith and agreed to baptize him. Thus, he became the first convert in the Stockbridge mission.[39]

Sergeant soon settled into the community, and by November, was teaching at a school the Indians had built, which was attended by about twenty students. On November 25, Sergeant departed for Albany to discuss with the Mohawks who resided there, the possibility of their moving to Stockbridge, and to get an idea of their feelings regarding a mission. While he was absent, Stephen Williams persuaded Timothy Woodbridge of Springfield to come and continue the work that had been started, and to fill in for Sergeant who had to return to Yale for the winter to complete his obligations there. Sergeant returned on November 30 and was confident that Woodbridge was well qualified to "…

---

[38] Hopkins, *Historical Memoirs*, 6.
[39] Hopkins, *Historical Memoirs*, 8–9.

take care of the School and to instruct the *Indians* in a Catechetical Way."[40] The first major trial for the new mission came almost immediately, however, and just as Sergeant was getting ready to return to Yale. Some Dutch traders had come to the area and sold rum to the Indians, which precipitated a drinking binge which lasted several days. When it came to the Sabbath meeting on Sunday December 8, the majority of the Indians still had not recovered and his audience was sparse. Sergeant was disheartened and angry. He recorded:

> This was the most discouraging Week I had. For the *Dutch* Traders, I was told had been very industrious to discourage the *Indians* from being *Christians*, thinking it would lessen their Trade with them, or at least they should not be under so good Advantages to cheat and oppose upon them. For they make vast Profit selling them *Rum*, and making Bargains with them when they are drunk; and Drunkenness is a Vice the Indians are extremely addicted to. The Traders tell them, that the *Religion* we are about to teach them, is not a good one; that we design in the End to serve ourselves by them, to make Slaves of them and their Children, and the like.[41]

The traders also tried to deceive the Indians by telling them that the laws forbidding the colonists from selling them rum was just another ploy of the government to take away the Indians' freedoms. The Indians were convinced by the trader's lies. Lieut. Umpachenee was upset, but his brother, who was a prominent tribal leader, was especially infuriated. Sergeant, hoping to leave them the next day, called a meeting with Umpachenee and Konkapot, who had not indulged in the drinking spree. He explained to them that the traders had lied to them and that they knew the negative effects that alcohol had on their people. The traders used that knowledge, he explained, to take unfair advantage of them while in a compromised state of mind. As proof of the trader's lies about the government removing their freedom by restricting the

---

[40] Hopkins, *Historical Memoirs*, 14.
[41] Hopkins, *Historical Memoirs*, 15.

sale of rum, Sergeant pointed out that the government had issued commissions to legitimate sellers and that through them the prices were fair, unlike the practices of the traders who came to them. The leaders were satisfied with his explanation. Sergeant stated, "With what I said they seem'd well satisfied, especially *Kunkapot*; for he saw thro' the Designs of the Traders."[42] Further evidence that the leaders trusted Sergeant and his explanation came the next day, for when he departed to return to New Haven, his travelling companions were Konkapot's nine-year-old son, Nungkawwat, and Umpachenee's eight-year-old son, Etowaukaum. Etowaukaum was the grandson of Chief Etowaukaum, who had travelled to England in 1710 to meet with Queen Anne. The boys were to spend the winter with Sergeant at Yale and begin their English and religious education.

On December 10, Sergeant wrote to the Indians, informing them that he was praying for them and encouraging them to stay true to the faith, and to avoid the vices to which they were being exposed. They received the letter gladly, especially since they were about to meet with the larger group of Hudson River Indians to gain acceptance and approval for the new mission. Capt. John Ashley (1669–1759), of Westfield, and Stephen Williams attended this meeting, which saw about 200 natives in attendance. Also present was the chief sachem Mtohksin, or Metoxen. At first, the Hudson River group was unhappy that a minister had been called and a school begun without their consent. Williams then gave a sermon to "one of the gravest, and most attentive Auditories that I ever preached to."[43] Afterwards he read a letter from John Stoddard, which served to answer any objections that the Indians may have had to the mission. It appears that the meeting was a success, for Williams recorded that

> they thanked us for the Pains we had taken, and desir'd Mr. *Woodbridge* might continue among them (at *Housatunnuk*)

---

[42] Hopkins, *Historical Memoirs*, 15–16.
[43] Quoted in Wheeler, *To Live*, 37.

and that Mr. SERGEANT would return to them; and said they would give an Account to their several *Towns*, of what we had offer'd to them: And gave us Encouragement that they would as a Nation submit to Instruction.[44]

Another cloud was soon to descend on the meeting, however, for after the affairs were concluded, the Indians had a great celebration, and the rum flowed freely. Subsequently, a number of the Indians fell ill, and two of them died; one being Umpachenee's brother-in-law. Rumor and conjecture among the Indians was that there had been a plot, by some against the mission, to poison Umpachenee and Konkapot. In a letter the two leaders sent to Rev. Nehemiah Bull they stated that opponents of the mission among the other Indian groups mocked the Housatonics for wanting to be like the English. The chiefs assured Bull that they were resolved to continue with the plan, stating, "they hate us for what we have Done but we don't intend to give out."[45] In all of these dealings, Sergeant was being kept informed, and in February, Ebenezer Poohpoonuc went to visit him in New Haven to give him an update and report on the general meeting that had been held. Sergeant sent a letter back with him, stating his joy that they desired to continue in the Way:

> But the greatest Pleasure of all is that, you have it yet in your Hearts to become *Christians*—When I had heard, that you concluded in your late general Meeting to embrace *Christianity*, it was more pleasing to me than cold Water to a thirsty Man in the Heat of Summer ...[46]

On July 1, 1735, Sergeant completed his obligation to Yale, and left New Haven to return to the Mohicans on the Housatonic on July 5. Immediately after arriving, he took up his post as teacher at both

---

[44] Hopkins, *Historical Memoirs*, 22.
[45] Wheeler, *To Live*, 38.
[46] Hopkins, *Historical Memoirs*, 25.

Wnahktakook and Skatehook schools, alternating between them with Timothy Woodbridge. The fledgling mission was immediately to undergo another trial of faith, however, as on July 15, some of the men ventured to New York territory to assist the Dutch with a harvest. Without doubt, they would have access to rum. There was serious concern back home and many prayed for their strength to withstand the temptation. "Capt. Konkapot was constantly bathed in tears; and when the laborers returned during the week, they were found to have endured beyond expectation. One man in particular, W-naum-pee, had resolutely held his ground, saying that he "designed to go to heaven, and must break off from such wickedness."[47] It appears that the Spirit of God was stirring the hearts of the Mohicans.

By June of 1735, it was evident to Sergeant that the hearts of the people were with him and that they had a true desire to embrace the Christian faith. A number of them, most notably Capt. Konkapot, had been examined and found ready to be baptized. The only issue was that Sergeant, while commissioned to go, had not yet been ordained and therefore could not perform any sacraments. On June 3, he wrote to the Rev. Dr. Colman, one of the Commissioners in Boston, wherein he recounted the great success the mission was experiencing and how accepting the Indians were of him. He reiterated his commitment to them and said, "I am very willing (if the Gentlemen *Commissioners* please) to devote my Life to the Service of their Souls."[48] He goes on to explain that there is plenty of work for two, and asks that Timothy Woodbridge be allowed to assist him. Additionally, he states that he had supported, out of his own resources, the two young Mohican boys who had wintered with him at Yale, and subsequently requested that the stipend of £100 be reviewed. At this point, he gets to the real reason for his letter: "Some of the *Indians* (I perceive) have a mind to be *baptiz'd*. Kunkapot,

---

[47] Jones, *Stockbridge*, 37.
[48] Hopkins, *Historical Memoirs*, 29.

especially, who appears to me well qualify'd for it. I have therefore tho't it would be convenient, I should be ordain'd speedily"[49]

On August 13, Sergeant received a letter from Adam Winthrop, Esq., on behalf of the Commissioners, informing him of their decision that he should be ordained as soon as possible. The date was set as Lord's Day, August 31, 1735, at Deerfield, the site of the 1704 massacre. When the day came and all the parties were assembled there must have been a sense of uneasiness on both sides, for some Indian participants in the massacre, and their survivors were in attendance:

> A number of survivors of that raid were present once again, meeting under very different circumstances. Caughnawagas and Schaghticokes had participated in the 1704 raid, and some of the participants may well have returned to Deerfield, now that peace had prevailed for over two decades. At least two of the English survivors were present, including Joseph Kellogg, who now served as interpreter, and the Reverend Stephen Williams. Both men had sisters who still remained among the Caughnawagas, living as Indians and Catholics.[50]

To show his support, Governor Belcher was also in attendance, and had asked the representatives of the various Indian groups with which they had made treaties to attend. At the ceremony, a sizeable group of Indians sat gravely taking in the proceedings. A preamble of the establishment of the Indian mission work was given by Rev. William Williams of Hatfield, followed by an ordination sermon, preached by Rev. Nathaniel Appleton (1693–1784). After being reminded of the charge being given him by the Governor and Commissioners and his acceptance of the charge, Sergeant was ordained. After the "Fellowship of El-

---

[49] Hopkins, *Historical Memoirs*, 29.
[50] Wheeler, *To Live*, 41.

ders," Rev. Stephen Williams, through an interpreter, asked the Indians if they would accept Sergeant as their minister, "To which they manifested their Willingness by rising up."[51]

It seems the timing was right for the mission, for when Sergeant took up his post with them on October 26, he immediately began to see the results of his ministry among the Mohicans. He spoke to Konkapot and his wife regarding baptism, and during the following week met with him and his family at their home in preparation.

> Accordingly, *Lord's-Day*, November 2d, I *baptiz'd Kunkapot* by the name of *John*, his Wife, *Mary*, and eldest Daughter. The Rest of the Children were not present, by Reason of the Badness of the weather. The Candidates shew'd a serious Sense of what they were about. It was done in the Presence of a considerable Number, both of *Christians*, and *Heathen*.[52]

Ebenezer Poohpoonuc, the mission's first baptismal candidate, then asked to be married as a Christian, so on November 7, Ebenezer and Sarah were married. The following Sunday, Sergeant baptized the remainder of Konkapot's children and Ebenezer's son. Then Umpachenee and his wife approached Sergeant about baptism. Sergeant tells us, "*Lord's-Day November 16th*. I *baptiz'd* the *Lieutenant* by the name of *Aaron*, his Wife, *Hannah* and the Rest of his family; as also the *Lieutenant's Wife's sister*, and *Ebenezer's Wife*; in all, eleven persons."[53] The trend continued and on the following Sunday, Sergeant baptized another eleven individuals, among whom was Umpachenee's brother, Tohtohkukhoonant. On December 7, he baptized another nine people. Sergeant recorded, "About this Time, the *Indians* agreed to have no Trading in *Rum*; which they remained by."[54] A pivotal point came on January 18, 1736, as Sergeant tells us that he preached at

---

[51] Hopkins, *Historical Memoirs*, 33.
[52] Hopkins, *Historical Memoirs*, 35.
[53] Hopkins, *Historical Memoirs*, 35.
[54] Hopkins, *Historical Memoirs*, 37.

Umpachenee's home to an audience of eighty or ninety souls, half of whom were from neighboring Indian villages. Afterwards he took time to talk with them more about the Christian faith, and their response was very favorable. "I heard some of the elderly Persons expres'd themselves much in Favour of the Christian Religion; wish'd our *Indians* might go on and prosper: and some said, they would come and live here."[55] The message of the gospel was taking hold among the Housatonic people.

Establishment of Stockbridge

The seasonal migration of the Housatonic peoples, however, made it difficult not only for them physically but spiritually as well.[56] There was a desire among Christian leaders that the Indians should be brought into a settled community to give some stability to their lives, allow for their learning of farming skills and animal husbandry, and more importantly, for the feeding of their minds and souls. Hopkins recorded,

> There was therefore, from the Beginning, a Design to accommodate them with Land, that they might all settle in one Place; and that there might be Accommodations, also for other of the *Tribe*, who might be dispos'd to come and settle with them.[57]

On February 10, Major Ebenezer Pomeroy (1669–1754) and Mr. Thomas Ingersole met with the Mohicans to discuss a plan of relocation. John Stoddard was unable to join them, as his mother was seriously ill.

Though the desired lands for their relocation were held by some English and Dutch settlers, after some negotiations a tract five miles square was procured. The resettlement would provide the integration

---

[55] Hopkins, *Historical Memoirs*, 37.
[56] Hopkins, *Historical Memoirs*, 43.
[57] Hopkins, *Historical Memoirs*, 43.

of four English families with the Indians and the land allotment included a portion assigned to John Sergeant and Timothy Woodbridge. "By the Grant of the *General Assembly*, Mr. Sergeant, their *Minister*, and Mr. *Woodbridge*, their *School-Master*, were made Proprietors, each of a sixtieth Part of the Township; and four *English* Families besides were to be accommodated with such a Part as the *Committee* should see fit."[58]

Subsequently, Stoddard, Ingersole and Pomeroy, met with the Mohicans, who still had some misgivings regarding the intentions of the English and the behavior of many so-called Christians. Konkapot was particularly concerned about why the English, having neglected them for so long, now were suddenly interested in their welfare, and wondered if there was not some ulterior motive behind it all. One of the major concerns he voiced was " if the Christian religion was so true and good, as he esteem'd it to be, how there should be so many Professors of it, who liv'd such vicious Lives and so contrary to what he was told, were the Rules of it."[59] Stoddard attempted to answer his objections, and in the end, the Mohicans seemed satisfied and agreed to proceed with the relocation plan. As to the Christian faith, Konkapot declared his commitment to it and stated that he was ready to die for his faith.[60]

With the completion of negotiations with the Mohicans and the ratification by the General Court in Boston, the town of Stockbridge was founded, named after Stockbridge in Hampshire, England. Despite the seeming amicability of negotiations, however, this was just the beginning of a clever plan to ultimately take control of Indian lands and move them out. "The meetings between the committee and Housatonic representatives reveal a pattern that would continue throughout the history of the mission: an act of purported benevolence became a means of acquiring yet more land from the Indians."[61]

---

[58] Hopkins, *Historical Memoirs*, 47.
[59] Hopkins, *Historical Memoirs*, 49.
[60] Hopkins, *Historical Memoirs*, 50.
[61] Wheeler, *To Live*, 55.

By January of 1737, Woodbridge completed his house and moved in with his wife. Sergeant boarded with them until April, at which time he went courting for his own wife. Originally, he had been attempting to woo Hannah Edwards, daughter of his Yale tutor, Jonathan Edwards, who would eventually be his successor in the Stockbridge mission work. He began a correspondence with her in 1735, a month before he was ordained, and tried, in vain, for two years to convince her to be his wife and join him in the mission. By April of 1737, however, he realized the relationship was not to be. While none of Hannah's letters have survived, Sergeant's are on file at the Beinecke Rare Book and Manuscript Library at Yale University, in New Haven, Connecticut. Fortuitous to his situation was the fact that one of the four families who chose to settle in Stockbridge in the summer of 1738 was that of Ephraim Williams. Sergeant was smitten with Abigail, Ephraim's young daughter, and the two were married on August 16, 1739. In a letter to Dr. Colman, he said,

> You will forgive me, Sir, if I think that most ingenious Woman—is not the smallest Gift of divine Bounty, that I have receiv'd, since I undertook a life tho't to be so self-denying. The more tenderly I love her, the more thankful I am to Heaven, who had form'd her as if on Purpose for me, and given her to me, as if, (like the Father of Mankind) he tho't it *not good for me to be here alone.*[62]

Abigail, being used to the finer things in a New England household, refused to live among the Indian settlement, and subsequently they built their own house on Prospect Hill, near her father Ephraim's house, overlooking the town.[63]

---

[62] Hopkins, *Historical Memoirs*, 78.
[63] Their home, Mission House, survives and today stands on the main street of Stockbridge, Mass.

*Mission House.
John & Abigail Sergeant's home-Stockbridge, Massachusetts*

They would have three children; Electa (1740-1798); Erastus (1743-1814), and John (Jr.) (1747-1824). Electa would marry Col. Mark Hopkins, Erastus would become a medical doctor, and John Jr. would become a minister and, later, a pastor to the Mohicans after their move to New Stockbridge, New York.

The initial work of Sergeant met with some measure of success. There were some professions of faith, baptisms, and a number of the Indians even started to build colonial style homes to live in, and to plant crops and keep animals to sustain themselves. More Indians were moving into the area, either to hear the Word of God, or to have their children educated in English ways. Frazier tells us, "Twenty Indian houses would go up in the next nine years."[64] Numerically, however, the Mohicans were suffering. The diseases that the English brought spread like wildfire through the settlement, and infant mortality was very high: "In 1740 there were 120 Indians in the town. Measuring births against deaths, though, the Mohican population had decreased. This was the hardest strain on Mohican culture. For several years the infant mortality rate was about 50 percent."[65]

Umpachenee's wife, Hannah, eventually contracted tuberculosis and suffered terribly. Just prior to her death on July 14, 1740, she spent the last days encouraging her husband and children to pursue godliness. She asked Sergeant to pray with her and declared to him that "she was content to die, hoping by that Means to be free from Sin, which was now her Burden, and if her Life was lengthen'd, out, it was likely, thro' Temptation, she should be prevailed upon to commit more Sin."[66] In March of 1741, Konkapot's wife Mary, who had also contracted tuberculosis, died. Hopkin's quoted from Sergeant's diary: "*March* the 29th. This evening (says Mr. Sergeant) died *Kunkapot's* wife, having enjoyed, all along in her sickness, a good Hope thro' Grace of a happy Eternity."[67] John himself would die in Stockbridge in 1766.

---

[64] Frazier, *The Mohicans*, 52.
[65] Frazier, *The Mohicans*, 52.
[66] Hopkins, *Historical Memoirs*, 83.
[67] Hopkins, *Historical Memoirs*, 83.

John Konkapot's grave in the Stockbridge Town Cemetery

During this period, two additional English families came to settle in the area. They were Joseph Woodbridge, Timothy's older brother, along with his wife and eight children, and Samuel Brown, a tailor, and deacon of the church in Watertown. The other two families, who had already been in Stockbridge for three years, were those of Ephraim Williams and Josiah Jones, Williams's brother-in-law. From all appearances the Stockbridge experiment was going well. By the mid-1740s there was strong evidence of urbanization and, besides the housing, there was a gristmill, a sawmill, and the presence of cultivated trees, crops, and grazing livestock. But all was not peace and harmony in the community. There were issues with the school and how it was being operated. Traders were still trying to take advantage of the Mohicans by forcing alcohol on them and the English settlers were beginning to swindle the Indians out of their properties. Umpachenee had taken to drinking excessively and was becoming difficult for Sergeant to deal with and eventually, as interactions with Umpachenee continued to deteriorate, he threatened to excommunicate the chief. Wheeler states that according to the records of the Moravian Mission, Umpachenee was excommunicated in 1741.[68] The chief ultimately was reconciled to Sergeant and the church. Frazier notes:

> Less than a year after these events John Sergeant wrote that "many notorious drunkards seem entirely to have broke off from their beloved strong drink, and of their own accord, and some the most unlikely to human appearance have resolved to taste no more strong drink, among whom Lieun. [Umpachenee] is one and is again reconciled to our conversion, and we begin to conceive of good hopes for him, tho' we are not altogether without fears."[69]

Sergeant's ministry was challenging, and he struggled between anxieties over the mission's funding as well as having to deal with conflicts between the Indians and settlers over land and property ownership. As Wheeler states, "Within a few years, any initial optimism Sergeant had once harbored had evaporated."[70] Sergeant had already admitted before going into the work that it would entail severe hardship for him, both physically and spiritually. Some of the hurdles he encountered may well have been the fact that, despite the good intentions of integrating the Mohicans and the English into a cohesive society, the Indians were still treated as inferiors and viewed as uncultured. We must hear from Sergeant's own record to ascertain his feelings about the Mohicans:

> I know not how to give any further *Satisfaction* for the present, than to *declare solemnly* that I have *no other Aim*, than the *Good of the Indians*, and that I have no Expectation of any *per-*

---

[68] Wheeler, *To Live*, 291, n.80
[69] Frazier, *The Mohicans*, 54.
[70] Wheeler, *To Live*, 60.

sonal Benefit at all, more than the *meer* [sic] *Satisfaction* of being *instrumental* under God, of doing them so great a *Kindness*, and rendering them a more *happy Society* by cultivating *Humanity* and Vertue [sic] among them.

That the *Indians*, in general, are a People *difficult* to be reformed from their own *foolish*, barbarous, and wicked Customs, the *Unsuccessfulness* of Attempts upon them for this Purpose is a melancholly [sic] *Proof*, which though it may appear *discouraging in further* Endeavours; yet, I think to a generous Mind it should rather be improved as *an Argument and form and Execute new Projections* for this Purpose. And indeed, perhaps, the *Neglect of promoting Industry* among them is the chief *moral Reason* of so *little* being to purpose in forming their Manners.[71]

Despite Sergeant's disappointment with the progress and success of the mission, he remained faithful to his charges, praying for them constantly and preaching to them the truth of God's Word. In early July, 1749 Sergeant came down with "a nervous fever, attended with canker," that lasted about twenty days. During his illness the Indians kept a vigil at the church, fasting and praying on his behalf. He died on July 27, 1749, at the age of thirty-nine.

---

[71] Hopkins, *Historical Memoirs*, 99.

*John and Abigail Sergeant's graves.
Stockbridge Town Cemetery*

The Mission Continues

After the loss of their beloved pastor, the next couple of years were unsettled for the Mohicans. In the interim, Rev. Stephen Williams and Rev. Samuel Hopkins would visit intermittently and bring spiritual guidance. As well, some Moravian missionaries began to minister to them and Umpachenee in particular was moved by their kindness. In 1751, however, he too fell ill and died on August 10, having remained true to his declaration of faith and sobriety about which Sergeant had expressed some doubt. In speaking of the evil effects of alcohol on the Indians, Hopkins recorded,

> the Lieutenant himself, who appear'd so zealous against that Vice, and seem'd to be firmly fix'd in the Ways of Religion, conducted himself in a very disorderly Manner, for a Year or

two together, being frequently intoxicated, and very troublesome: But he was afterwards recover'd from his Apostacy [*sic*]; confessed his Wickedness; and was restored to Charity; and walked orderly to the day of his death"[72]

The period of 1749–1751 was especially troublesome for the Mohicans as, without a strong advocate on their behalf, the English, in particular the family of Ephraim Williams, began to posture and connive to secure more lands and control the local political situation. Two days prior to Umpachenee's death, Sergeant's replacement, Jonathan Edwards (1703–1758) assumed the pulpit and ministry to the Indians and whites in Stockbridge. His appointment was strongly opposed by Abigail Sergeant and the Williams family, who were cousins of Edwards. Details of this period are more fully covered in the later section on Jonathan Edwards. Suffice it to say at this point that Edwards was a classic Puritan preacher who did not mince words when it came to addressing sin and salvation. He was also not a particularly sociable individual. However, he cared very deeply for his Indian charges and became their strongest advocate during this period, and would protect them from being swindled by the whites.

Following Edwards' move to assume the presidency of Princeton University in 1758, Rev. Stephen West became the pastor to the Stockbridge residents. From the outset, however, it became clear that West was not committed to the welfare of the Mohican people, demonstrated by the fact that he had married into the Williams family. During this time, some of the Indian men who had gone off to fight for the Crown in the French and Indian War during Edwards' ministry, were now returning to the community. Frazier notes,

> When the Stockbridge heroes returned home, they found a new minister. Stephen West was another Yale man and an old-guard Calvinist, long on Christian exactitude and discipline, short on Christian compassion. He seems to have had

---

[72] Hopkins, *Historical Memoirs*, 159.

only one special credential to head the Indian mission. He, too, had married one of the Williams girls.[73]

During this time there was also an unsuccessful move to separate the white and Indian congregations. West's reasons for supporting such a proposal centred on the fact that he could not speak Mohican, and therefore could not adequately minister to the Indians. As well, he did not have enough time to prepare sermons for both groups: "In more than fifteen years as minister among the Indians of Stockbridge, he baptized forty-nine children but admitted only twenty-two Indians to full communion with the church, all but one of them women."[74] He was also becoming increasingly harsh towards the Indians in his congregation and began to enforce strict discipline toward them. By early 1773, West had excommunicated every last Indian from his congregation. In November, the Commissioners in Boston removed him as the Indians' pastor, however, he continued to preach to the English in the community. His replacement, John Sergeant Jr., was trained in theology and ministry under the tutelage of West, and could speak Mohican, though he was not ordained. Like his father, he was humble and committed, and became the teacher at the mission school to the Indians. He once stated, "For I am altogether unworthy; and an unlikely means of doing any good in the Lord's vineyard."[75]

Another major blow to the Indians came in 1776 with the start of the Revolutionary War, as many of the Indian men enlisted to fight for the American colony. Upon their return, however, they found their lands were forfeit due to debt or unscrupulous deals, and petitioned the New York General Assembly to intervene, reminding them of their mutual aid to each other in times of need. Their petition reads like a dirge:

> Brothers, wise Men! When you first came over the great water to this our Island, you was small, I was great. I then had

---

[73] Frazier, *The Mohicans*, 138.
[74] Frazier, *The Mohicans*, 188.
[75] Quoted in Frazier, *The Mohicans*, 190.

a fullness of food and cloathing [*sic*], I then was happy and contented. The sands and waters of this River, which you now possess were mine, that is those on the east side of it. Here I got my food and cloathing. You being them smaller I invited you to set down with me, and provide for yourself, your women and children. This you did. We were then happy in each other, your enemies were my enemies, your friends were my friends. Where you bled by the hatchet of your enemies, there I bled also, for you and your friends. Where your fathers died in battle, my fathers died by their side. The waters of Lake George and Champlain, the hills about Boston and New York bear witness to this. The last time you took up the hatchet against the French King I went out with you with my hatchet, there I was with all my warriors many years.

The rewards for this service given to your warriors in land, were not given to mine. When I returned I found my hunting grounds ruined. You get food and cloathing by tilling the earth. I by killing wild beasts on my ancient hunting ground, they can now find no hiding places. You til it all. Some land my fathers told me they had given you, much they told me they had not given you. What they gave you not is still mine by the customs and laws of all nations. The great Spirit gave my fathers this what he has not taken away by conquest, and I or my fathers have not alienated, either by gift or sale, is certainly in the view of that Spirit, mine still.

This I related to my brothers the Bostonians who had also in their possession some of my land, they acknowledged my rights, and gave me full compensation. My claims are from Hudson River, Wood Creek and Lake Champlain, to the mouth of Otter Creek on the north eastward.

Now Brethren; wise men; attend. You once was small, very small. I then was great at that time. I took you under my arm, and helped you. I am now become small, very small. You are become great, very great, you reach into the clouds. You are seen all over the world. I am not now high as your ankles. I now look to you for help. I am weak through hunger and cold, through want of food and cloathing. My women groan and lament, and tears are in the eyes of all my children.

> Brother! What I ask is that you resign to me that land, which is justly mine, which I have neither sold or given to you; or give me its value, that I may get food and cloathing for myself, my women and children and be happy with you as formerly; Remember too, that by this you will not leave room for lying birds to say, that you neglect to do me justice, because you are strong. Brothers, should you give me anything, let it be given in such a manner, that men of evil minds may not deprive me, who am weak, of it justly.[76]

No record exists to indicate whether this petition was ever received or responded to. After a series of failed attempts to get any sort of justice from the government, the Mohicans accepted an offer of a six square mile tract of land from the Oneidas in New York and decided to relocate. In 1784, the majority of the Indians moved to a community they called New Stockbridge, with about forty stragglers arriving in 1788. John Sergeant Jr. continued to minister to the Mohicans, travelling back and forth between the two Stockbridges, until 1796 when he moved his family to New Stockbridge permanently. During this time, Samson Occom, a Mohegan Indian and an ordained minister, came to the area, and tensions rose between the two men. The result was a dispute between them which, in 1788, split the Mohican church. Occom's sudden death in 1792, however, led to the reunification of the two congregations. During the following years, white encroachment was once again forcing Indians everywhere to seek new lands to the West. Hendrick Aupaumut, a Mohican chief who had been a faithful warrior in the army and of whom it was said that George Washington had personally presented him with a Captain's sword, managed to procure land for the tribe on the White River in Indiana from the Delaware and Miami tribes. In 1818, a group of families set out for the new lands in Indiana, however, before they arrived, the lands were transferred to the federal government. An appeal to authorities fell on deaf ears and the majority

---

[76] Frazier, *The Mohicans*, 234–235.

of the Mohicans returned, despondent and discouraged, to New Stockbridge. Another delegation was sent to Wisconsin in 1821 and was successful in obtaining property along the Fox River from the Menominee and Winnebago tribes. As the funds became available, the Mohicans once more began a western migration: "A group of 30 reached Green Bay in the summer of 1824, another of about 50 left New York in 1825. In 1827, Captain Hendrick's wife, Lydia, purchased the meetinghouse and its one-acre lot. Finally, in 1829, the aging Captain Hendrick himself made the journey to Green Bay, where he died the next year."[77] Sergeant continued to minister to his flock until his death in New Stockbridge on September 9, 1824.

On May 30, 1830, President Andrew Jackson signed into law one of the most infamous pieces of legislation in United States history: The Indian Removal Act. The purpose of this act was to relocate all native tribes west of the Mississippi River and was nothing short of genocide for many of the Indian people. The 1830s were also a tumultuous and discordant time for the Mohicans as a rebel group, the Emigrant Party, began to sow serious seeds of discord. During this period, the leaders of the Emigrant Party invited in about two hundred migrant Munsee Indians, which resulted in a conflict that saw a number of Emigrant families moving to Kansas in 1839. To further complicate the Mohicans' lives, two political factions developed within the tribe. There was the "Indian Party," who wanted to maintain tribal government and hold their lands, and the "Citizen Party," who supported becoming citizens of the United States, which would allow them to vote and use the courts in exchange for relinquishing their Indian status and land claims. This rift in the tribe would continue for about fifty years.[78] Finally, in 1856, a treaty was signed which gave the Mohicans two townships in the southwest corner of the Menominee reservation in Shawano

---

[77] Lion J. Miles, "1784–1829 The Tribe Leaves New York," https://www.mohican.com/history-1784-1829-the-tribe-leaves-new-york/ (accessed August 14, 2019).

[78] Siemers, *Proud and Determined*, 111.

County, Wisconsin.[79] The Stockbridge Mohicans would become the Stockbridge-Munsee Band of Mohicans. They remain there to this day with about 1500 enrolled tribal members, 800 of which live on or near the reservation.

Indian Burial Ground. Main Street Stockbridge, Massachusetts. Inscription reads, "The Ancient Burial Place Of The Stockbridge Indians 1734. The Friends Of Our Fathers 1877"

---

[79] James Oberle, *A Nation of Statesmen: The Political Culture of the Stockbridge-Munsee Mohicans, 1815-1972* (Norman: University of Oklahoma Press, 2005), 256–263.

2
Muh-he-ca-ne-ok— Their Spirituality

"For ever since the world was created, people have seen the earth and sky. Through everything God made, they can clearly see his invisible qualities—his eternal power and divine nature. So they have no excuse for not knowing God." (Romans 1:20, NLT)

The Native American tribes were monotheistic, having belief in both a benevolent "Great, Good Spirit," and an evil spirit, who was responsible for the corruption that was evident around them. The Mohicans were a spiritual people, with a sort of catechism and rule of family religious order that was to be practiced daily, and passed from generation to generation. In order to demonstrate their devoutness, it is important to recount an abbreviated description of their faith as given by Mohican historian, Chief Hendrick Aupaumut.[1] He recorded:

> Our ancestors, before they ever enjoyed Gospel revelation acknowledged one Supreme Being who dwells above, whom they styled Waun-theet Mon-nit-toow, or the Great Good Spirit, the author of all things in heaven and on earth, and also believed that there is an evil one, called, Mton-toow or Wicked Spirit, that loves altogether to do mischief: that he excites person or persons to tell a lie—angry, fight, hate steal, to commit murder, and to be envious, malicious, and evil-talking, also excites nations to war with one another, to violated their friendship which the Great, Good Spirit given

---

[1] To be true to his record, spelling and grammar have been left unchanged.

them to maintain for their mutual good, and their children after them.

In Order to please the Great, Good Spirit which they acknowledged to be their dependence, and on the other to withstand the evil one—therefore, the following custom was observed, which handed down to them by their forefathers, and considered as communicated to them by Good Spirit.

The Head of each family—man or woman—would begin with all tenderness, as soon as daylight, to waken up their children and teach them as follows:

My Children—you must remember that it is by the goodness of the Great, Good Spirit we are preserved through the night. My children you must listen to my words. If you wish to see many good days and evenings you must love to all men, and be kind to all people.

If you see any that are in distress, you must try to help them. Remember you must give him something to eat; though you should have only a little cake, give him half of it, for you also liable to hunger. If you see one naked, you must cover him with your own raiment ...

My little Children, if you see aged man or woman on your way doing something, you must pity on them, and help them instantly. In so doing, you will make their hearts glad, and they will speak well of you. And further, if you see your neighbors quarreling, you must try to make them to be good friends again. And you must always listen to the instructions of old folks: thereby you will be wise. And you must not be hasty to speak, when you hear people talking, nor allow yourself too much laughing. ... But live in peace with all people: thereby you will please the Great, Good Spirit, and you will be happy. My little Children—you must be very kind to strangers. If you see stranger or strangers come by the side of your fireplace, you must salute them, and take them by the hand, and be friendly to them: because you will be a stranger sometime or other. ...

My Children—again listen. You must be honest in all your ways. You must always speak nothing but the truth wherever you are. ...

Their Spirituality

> My Children—you must never steal anything from your fellow men, for remember this—you will not be pleased if some of your neighbors should take away your things by way of stealing: and you must also remember that the Great, Good Spirit see you. ...
>
> My Children—you must always avoid bad company. And above all *you* must never commit murder, because you wish to see long life. But if you commit murder, the Great, Good Spirit will be angry with you, and your life will be in great danger, also the life of your dear relations.
>
> My Children—you must be very industrious. You must always get up early morning to put on your clothes, muk-sens, and tie your belt about you, that you may be ready to do something; by so doing you will always have something to eat and to put on. But if you will be lazy, you will always be poor. ... And further, my Children—when you grown up, you must not take wife or husband without the consent of your parents, and all relations. But if you will do contrary to this, perhaps you will be joined to one who will bring great darkness to you, and thereby you will be very unhappy.
>
> My Children—at all times you must obey your Sachem and Chiefs, in all good counsels they give; never to speak evil against them, for they have taken much pains in promoting your happiness. And if you do not observe this, you will be looked upon worse than the beast are.
>
> Thus they inculcate instruction to their children day after day until they are grown up; and after they are grown, yet they would teach them occasionally. And when young people have children they also teach it to theirs in like manner.— This custom is handed down from generation to another ...[2]

Reading this rule of faith and practice, one cannot but be impressed with how many of its principles can be directly linked to Biblical commands. As a short exercise, the Mohican rule and a few applicable corresponding Scripture passages will be compared.

---

[2] Bernd C. Peyer, ed., *American Indian Nonfiction: An Anthology of Writings, 1760s–1930s* (Norman: University of Oklahoma Press, 2017), 66–68.

The first command, to rise early and teach the children, is remarkably similar to Deuteronomy 6:6-7, "These commandments that I give you today are to be on your hearts. Impress them on your children. Talk about them when you sit at home and when you walk along the road, when you lie down and when you get up." The admonition to love and be kind to all people can also be found throughout Scripture, most notably in Leviticus 19:18; John 13:35-35; 1 John 4:7-8; 1 Corinthians 16:14, and Colossians 3:14. The instruction to aid those in distress can be found in numerous passages, with Deuteronomy 15:11; Proverbs 22:9; Matthew 5:42; Matthew 25:35-40, and Hebrews 13:16 being just a few instances. As for acting as a peacemaker when you see neighbors in disagreement, Scripture provides the same directions in Matthew 5:9; Romans 12:18; 2 Corinthians 13:11, and Hebrews 12:14. As to the importance of listening to instruction from elders, the book of Proverbs contains many references to the wisdom of such a practice. Treating strangers with kindness can be found in Proverbs 25:21; Hebrews 13:2, 6, and 1 Peter 4:9. The Mohican instruction to be truthful and honest is addressed specifically in the eighth commandment, found in Exodus 20:16, with additional references in Proverbs 6:17; 12:17; 14:5; 16:11, and Leviticus 19:36. Guidance against theft and murder are also covered explicitly as commandments six and eight in Exodus 20:1-17. The command to be industrious has Biblical equivalents in Proverbs 6:6-12; 12:24; 14:23; 21:5; Galatians 6:9, and 2 Thessalonians 3:10. As it pertains to marriage, there is strong biblical guidance regarding the importance of seeking counsel from parents and elders when seeking a wife; this can be seen in the fifth commandment (Exod. 20:12), and is echoed in Matthew 15:4; Mark 7:10; Luke 18:20, and Ephesians 6:2. Additional passages addressing the issue of marriage can be found in Deuteronomy 7:3-4, and 2 Corinthians 6:14-17, which both sternly advise against inappropriate marriages and warn of their ensuing dangers. Finally, we see the instruction to always obey those in authority paralleled in Romans 13:1-7, and 1 Peter 2:13-17.

The Mohicans also have a creation story which, at the beginning, is not dissimilar to the Genesis account of creation, and states that, "everything started out with nothing but black. A black wide open space, and within that space dwelt a being, not man nor woman but both, because both female and male makes life. This being is called Kiisheelumukweengw."[3] Another associated tribe's[4] creation story begins, "Long ago it was dark and nothing existed. Only the Great Spirit existed."[5]

When John Sergeant first came to the Housatonics they invited him to sit in on a sacrificial ceremony. The Indians first assembled at the wigwam of John Konkapot, and were seated around a makeshift altar. After Sergeant took his place, two men took down a recently killed deer which had been hanging in the centre of the lodge, and proceeded to skin and quarter it before finally reassembling the skin and meat on the altar "so as to make it look as much like a whole Deer as might be." At this point, an appointed elder stood and prayed loudly, "O great God, pity us, grant us food to eat, afford us good and comfortable sleep, preserve us from being devoured by the fowls that fly in the air. This deer is given in token that we acknowledge thee the giver of all things."[6] The elder who had prayed was then given a string of wampum as payment by the warrior who had killed the deer. The Indians then cut up the deer and boiled it before giving everyone, except the man who had killed it, a portion to eat. This act served to indicate that it was his gift to the tribe. Finally, an elderly needy widow was given the skin and insides to use for herself.

One can only speculate as to what "being devoured by the fowls that fly in the air" might be referring to in the elder's prayer—perhaps a reference to demons. What is obvious is that Sergeant missed the opportunity to point out the similarities between the Christian message of

---

[3] "Creation Story" by Jeremy Mohawk, Arvid E. Miller Memorial Museum and Archives, Bowler, WI.

[4] The Delaware Lenapes.

[5] "Stories of the Lenape People with translations in the Lenape Language" as told by Chief Robert Red Hawk Ruth, Lenape Nation of Pennsylvania. Library at Delaware Nation of Moraviantown, Thamesville, Ontario.

[6] Hopkins, *Historical Memoirs*, 12.

Christ's sacrifice, and their ceremony. Rather, he chose only to condemn it: "The above Historical Account I have not inserted so much for its being curious, as to excite Compassion towards such ignorant Creatures, and the charitable Endeavours of generous Minds to bring them out of such a benighted State."[7]

It would appear though, that despite condemning this ceremony, he did not enforce strict practices on the Mohicans, for he allowed them to continue other rituals and dances. This may have been due to the fact that Sergeant realized the Indians themselves acknowledged the futility of their pagan practices. Hopkins records, "Mr. Sergeant goes on and observes that the *Indians* us'd to have an high opinion of these *Pawwaws*, ... However, they confess they have no Power over *Christians*."[8]

Various stories and rumors abound in the history of the Housatonic area regarding the Indians having a pre-knowledge of the Scriptures. Jones stated, "The historian [Aupaumut], too informed Dr. West that his people once possessed the Good Book given by the Great Spirit; but that having lost the power to read it, they had buried it with a chief."[9] There is also the story of Joseph Merrick, Esq., of Pittsfield, Massachusetts who in 1815, while ploughing a field in an area known as "Indian Hill," turned up a hard, leather-bound packet containing pieces of parchment with Hebrew script on them. He states,

> On the parchment was written, in Hebrew characters, the identical passages of Scripture which the Jews used as Phylacteries, viz.: Ex. 13th, 11th to 16th, Deut. 6th, 4th to 9th, and 11th, 13th to 21st. In opening the case, Esq. M. destroyed one of the strips; the others were sent to the Antiquarian Society.[10]

---

[7] Hopkins, *Historical Memoirs*, 13.
[8] Hopkins, *Historical Memoirs*, 24.
[9] Jones, *Stockbridge*, 18–19.
[10] Jones, *Stockbridge*, 19. See also J. E. A. Smith, *History of Pittsfield, (Berkshire County), Massachusetts, From the year 1734 to the year 1800* (Boston: Lee and Shephard, 1869), 44.

Stories of similar finds among other tribes were also reported,[11] leading to the theory that perhaps the Native American Indians were some of the lost tribes of Israel.

As the tribe embraced Christianity, early teachings of the Protestant church were translated into the Mohican tongue. Oberle cites one such teaching. "One of the great cultural projects of the first decade at New Stockbridge was undertaken by Joseph Quinney and Hendrick Aupaumut in translating the Puritan 1648 "Westminster Assembly's Shorter Catechism" into Mohican."[12] To get a taste of the complexity of the Mohican language, one article of the catechism, with its translation, is provided:

Q.21. Who is the Redeemer of God's elect?
A. The only Redeemer of God's elect is the Lord Jesus Christ, who, being the eternal Son of God, became man, and so was, and continueth to be God and man, in two distinct natures, and one person, forever.[13]

Q.21. Owwauneck nuh puhquaukhkennaut Pohtommauwaus nootnauchee?
A. Nuk nun nqueheheh puhquaukhkennaut Pohtommauwaus nootnauchee Taupaunmowaut Jesus Christ, neen stoh eyuhquauyoqueh Pohtommauwaus wtiomun, nuh nooh autonnawusetup nun kuh neh wtennoinaup Pohtommauwausope, den unnenauqsooh aunow nooh autonnawutheet, psooqqueek huch pausqunnowope whukki honmeweh.[14]

In studying the legends, myths and practices of the Mohicans, it is easy to see how the many similarities between their beliefs and those contained in Scripture meant the missionaries had a firm foundation

---

[11] Jones, *Stockbridge*, Appendix C.
[12] Oberle, *A Nation*, 28.
[13] "The Westminster Shorter Catechism," https://bpc.org/wp-content/uploads/2015/06/d-scatechism.pdf (accessed, July 26, 2019).
[14] "The Assembly's Shorter Catechism," Arvid E. Miller Memorial Museum and Archives, Bowler, WI.

from which to start preaching. However, their previous dealings with government officials, which always led to the Mohicans' disadvantage, was soon to affect their spiritual lives as well.

The first amendment to the Constitution of the United States was passed by Congress on September 25, 1789 and ratified on December 15, 1791. It states, "Congress shall make no law respecting an establishment of religion, or prohibiting the free exercise thereof; or abridging the freedom of speech, or of the press; or the right of the people peaceably to assemble, and to petition the Government for a redress of grievances."[15] As if unfairly treating the Indians—taking their lands and forcing them to live on reservations residing on less than desirable land—was not sufficiently dehumanizing, the government would go a step further and also remove their religious freedom.

In a presentation to the Department of the Interior on December 2, 1882, Secretary I. M. Teller said:

> Sir: I desire to call your attention to what I regard as a great hindrance to the civilization of the Indians, viz, the continuance of the old heathenish dances, such as the sun-dance scalp-dance, &c. These dances, or feasts, as they are sometimes called, ought, in my judgement, to be discontinued, and if the Indians now supported by the Government are not willing to discontinue them, the agents should be instructed to compel such discontinuance.[16]

The result was that on March 30, 1883, the Court of Indian Offences was established, and the practice of Native religion declared illegal. The Commissioner of Indian Affairs, Hiram Price, signed the declaration which stated,

---

[15] https://www.govinfo.gov/content/pkg/GPO-CONAN-1992/pdf/GPO-CONAN-1992-10-2.pdf (accessed August 20, 2019).

[16] "Rules Governing The Court of Indian Offences," Arvid E. Miller Museum and Archives, Bowler, WI.

In compliance with the suggestions contained in the foregoing letter, the following rules are promulgated for the guidance and direction of the several United States Indian agents, and each agent will see to it that the requirements thereof are strictly enforced, with the view of having the evil practices mentioned by the honorable Secretary ultimately abolished.[17]

Any Indian caught practicing native rituals and dances would be faced with a thirty-day jail sentence. Also removed in this edict was the traditional role of the tribal medicine man with the result that the Indians had to practice many of their rites and customs in secret. This violation of Indian freedom remained in effect until August 11, 1978, when President Jimmy Carter signed into law the American Indian Religious Freedom Act which says:

Resolved by the Senate and House of Representatives of the United States of America in Congress assembled, That henceforth it shall be the policy of the United States to protect and preserve for American Indians their inherent right of freedom to believe, express, and exercise the traditional religions of the American Indian, Eskimo, Aleut, and Native Hawaiians, including but not limited to access to sites, use and possession of sacred objects, and the freedom to worship through ceremonials and traditional rites.[18]

Sadly, over the hundred years that the Mohicans lived under this religious persecution, many of the rich traditions and customs of the Indians would be lost forever. However, their faith in the Good Spirit would live on, with some of the Mohicans even today reciting the following prayer at the opening or closing of a meal.

---

[17] "Rules Governing The Court of Indian Offences," Arvid E. Miller Museum and Archives, Bowler, WI.

[18] U.S. Congress, Senate, Committee on Indian Affairs, *American Indian Religious Freedom Act, 95th Cong., 1978, S. Rept 95-709,* accessed August 20, 2019, https://www.govinfo.gov/content/pkg/STATUTE-92/pdf/STATUTE-92-Pg469.pdf.

> Anushiik kiisheelumukweengw eelu mox wulahkameek, anushiik weemu-kweekw wulutool peetuwuyeengw. Miixaskwal, mihtukwak, awehleeshooshak, waak aweeyayusak. Xwat-anushiik eelu miilkayeegw weemu yool miichwaakanal, waak noolamalusuwaakaniha. Xwat-anusiik eelu miilkayeengw ndihuluniixsuwaakanihna. Mehch-ngiish Pahtamawe.

> Thank you creator for this most beautiful day. Thank you for all the beautiful things you have brought us. Grasses, tree, birds and the animals. Big thank you for giving us all these foods and our good health. Big thank you for giving us our language. Now I'm done praying.[19]

Present State of Spirituality
In the wake of World War I, the roaring twenties would soon give way to the stock market crash, ushering in the decade of the dirty thirties. During this national economic disaster, Americans sought out whatever means they could to survive, which included turning to the church for help. Among the Mohicans, faith was also kindled anew. Oberly summarizes the situation on the reservation well:

> The Great Depression proved a fertile time for the propagation of the gospel among the Stockbridge-Munsees., both at the new settlement of Moh-he-con-nuck and at the older settlements, Red Springs, the Lutheran Mission, and Morgan Siding. The Lutherans of Morgan Siding, who had been meeting for decades in a schoolhouse, built their own Our Saviour's Lutheran Church in 1932. The Lutheran Mission had to close the boarding part of the school in 1933 because of a funding shortage, but the day school continued, as did the Immanuel Lutheran Church, the heart of the mission. ... The Presbyterians of the John Sergeant Memorial Church in Red Springs had dwindled to just a handful of members in the 1930s, when a crisis over personnel assignments in the presbytery prompted a walkout from the Presbyterian Church,

---

[19] *A Brief History*, 91.

U.S.A. Led by members of the Shepherd and Tousey families, the protesters established the Old Stockbridge Orthodox Presbyterian Church in Morgan Siding. [20]

Today, the spiritual needs of the Mohicans on the reservation in Wisconsin are provided by a number of congregations, including The Lutheran Church of the Wilderness; Stockbridge Bible Church; Old Stockbridge Orthodox Presbyterian Church; Our Saviour's Lutheran Church, and the Immanuel Mohican Indian Lutheran Church.

The Lutheran Church of the Wilderness is a member of the East-Central Synod of the Evangelical Lutheran Church in America. It was founded in 1936, and was affiliated with the Lutheran Church-Missouri Synod. Their website states, "The Congregation met in various buildings on the Reservation until the church was constructed in 1955. ... In 1981 Wilderness joined the Association of the Evangelical Lutheran Churches, later merging into the Evangelical Lutheran Church in America (ELCA)."[21] At the current time it has 286 baptized members and 117 confirmed members on the rolls, though regular worshippers average between 15-65. In terms of worship style, the Pastor comments:

> We regularly incorporate Native American phrasing (Creator instead of Father/God, Pohtahmawus as a Gender-inclusive name for Holy Spirit, Brother Jesus instead of Lord, etc.) and use certain Native American practices on a semi-regular basis. (Drum circles, Smudging with sage and sweet grass, Calling to the Four Directions, praying for Mother Earth and Father Sky, Blowing of the Conch Shell to gather for worship,

---

[20] Oberle, *A Nation*, 182

[21] "Our History," Lutheran Church of the Wilderness, accessed September 4, 2019, https://www.lutheranchurchofthewilderness.com/history.

offering tobacco to ancestors [including to the rivers/lakes/other bodies of water] and giving medicine/tobacco pouches).[22]

The Immanuel Mohican Indian Lutheran Church was founded in 1898, and in 1908 a mission school was built which operated until it was closed in 1958. Currently, there is an effort to restore the school as a historic site, though in recent years the church itself has experienced a decline in enrollment and attendance. In 2009, there were 60 baptized members, 40 communicants and an average attendance of 20. By 2017 there were only 20 baptized and communicant members, with an average attendance of 8-10 people at the services.[23] The last full-time pastor was Rev. Rolland Goltz. Sadly, this church is in danger of imminent closure.

The Old Stockbridge Orthodox Presbyterian Church is a member of the Orthodox Presbyterian Churches and, as they are a Reformed congregation, follow the regulative principle of worship. Currently, there are 20 communicant members and 4 non-communicant adherents. About half of the congregation are Mohican Indians.[24]

Our Saviour's Lutheran Church in Morgan Siding was founded in 1902. They began meeting in a private home, but in 1907, when the group became too large, moved to a local school house where they remained until 1931. The church building, where they still worship today, was dedicated on November 6, 1932.[25] The congregation is a member of the Lutheran Church Missouri Synod and has 60 baptized

---

[22] Email correspondence from Lutheran Church of the Wilderness Pastor Paul Andrew Johnson, August 18, 2019.

[23] The Lutheran Church Missouri Synod, http://locator.lcms.org/nchurches_frm/c_graphs.asp?C382025 (accessed September 4, 2019).

[24] Email correspondence from Old Stockbridge Orthodox Presbyterian Church pastor Micah Shin, September 7, 2019.

[25] Putnam, *Christian Religion*, 29.

members, 49 confirmed members and a weekly attendance of about 23. Their spiritual leader is Dr. Roy Rinehard.[26]

The Stockbridge Bible Church began with humble beginnings on April 14, 1977 in the home of Mrs. Ethel Doxtator. Its first official Sunday service was held on April 17, 1977, at the home of their Pastor, Gordon Shepard. The congregation then obtained a mobile home and, after being renovated, held its first Sunday service there on July 24, 1977. Despite several attempts at contact, the current status of the church could not be obtained.

---

[26] The Lutheran Church Missouri Synod, accessed September 11, 2019, http://locator.lcms.org/nchurches_frm/c_detail.asp?C382168.

3
THE STOCKBRIDGE BIBLE

In 1744, John Sergeant prepared a proposal and appeal for the funding of a boarding school in Stockbridge and sent it to Thomas Coram in England. Coram was a retired sea captain, and spent his retirement raising funds for benevolent causes. He was well connected to those with influence, especially among the reigning royal family, and familiar with the effective protocols needed to obtain support. Coram wrote up a petition for subscriptions and, hoping to gain the support of Frederick, the Prince of Wales, sent it through the proper channels. It began, "This Petition, with a Letter, and the Subscription Book, Capt. *Coram* sent to Col. John Shute, Privy Purse to His *Royal Highness*, with whom he was well acquainted ..."[1] Since Shute was unable to see the Prince, he sent it directly to the Rev. Dr. Francis Ayscough, who also happened to be the Prince's personal chaplain. Ayscough presented the petition and request to the Prince, who was the first to subscribe, accompanied with a gift of twenty guineas. Ayscough also decided to give a meaningful gift to the Mohicans and he sent a beautiful Bible in two volumes, which had been printed in London, in 1717 by the King's printer, John Baskett. Ayscough inscribed the following inside both volumes, "The gift of the Reverend D. Francis Ayscough to the Indian Congregation at Housatonic in New England MDCCXLV"[2] Coram also included a dedication:

---

[1] Samuel Hopkins, *Historical Memoirs, Relating to the Housatunnuk Indians* (Boston: S. Kneeland, 1753), 121.

[2] Jeffrey Siemers, *Proud and Determined: A History of the Stockbridge Mohicans, 1734-2014* (Fond du Lac, Wisconsin: Big Smokey Press, 2013), 162.

> This with another volume, containing the Holy Bible, is the pious gift of the Reverend Doct. Francis Ayscough, clerk of the closet to his Royal Highness Frederick, Prince of Wales, to the use of the congregation of Indians at or near Housatonic, in a vast wilderness, part of New England, who are, at present, in the voluntary Care, and Instruction, of the Learned and Religious Mr. John Sergeant, and is to remain to the use of the Successors of those Indians from Generation to Generation; as a testimony of the said doctor's Great Regard for the Salvation of their souls and is over and above other Benefits, which he most cheerfully obtained for the encouragement of the said Mr. Sergeant, and in favour of the said Indians.
> At the request of their hearty Friend and Well Wishes
>
> London,
> the 31st day of December, 1745. Thomas Coram

Sergeant received the donation and the Bible by May 20, 1746 and acknowledged receipt in a return letter to Ayscough, dated January 24, 1747.

> *Reverend Sir*, With great Satisfaction and much Gratitude, I receiv'd your most obliging Favour of *May* 20, 1746. Assuring me of your approving of my design. ...Your own Gift to our Congregation, I thankfully accept, both as an Instance of your Goodness and Piety. As it ever has been, so it will, I trust, still be, my zealous Endeavour to communicate to this poor People the pure Doctrines of God, and the Words of eternal Life, as they are contain'd in the holy Scriptures; ever praying that they may be made wise to Salvation by them.[3]

---

[3] Hopkins, *Historical Memoirs*, 124–125.

*Stockbridge Bible and Communion Set.
Photo courtesy The Arvid E. Miller Memorial Library Museum*

The Bible was considered a sacred trust by the Mohicans and it was revered by them whenever they moved. At some point a special wooden chest was built to protect it when it was not in use. We know it was present with them and in use in worship services when they moved to Wisconsin as Calvin Colton (1789-1857), a Presbyterian minister recorded:

> I saw a Bible yesterday, safely kept in a sort of ark, at their place of worship. (A remarkable relic of Hebrew custom), printed at Oxford ... And here it is, as bright and as perfect, as when first it came from the hands of the pious donor;—and that not to prove, that it has not been used—for it has been constantly used in public worship. But it has been *carefully* used, and carefully kept in the *ark of the covenant*! It came from *Old* England to the "Housatonic, in the vast wilderness of *New* England." It was transported with the tribe to the

State of New York;—and for aught I know, with all the sacerdotal solemnities of their Hebrew father, in ancient days. And it was again transported by the same religious care to *this* vast wilderness, of the North-West. And here it is: a perpetual monument of their fear of God, and of their love for his word and ordinances. Their reverence for this volume and for the ark, which contains it, is almost superstitious.[4]

The tribe had been served by the Presbyterian minister Jeremiah Slingerland, who had graduated from Bangor Theological Seminary and was himself a Mohican. With his death in 1884 the church began to falter and written accounts of the Bible's whereabouts are scarce. In 1907, there was strong desire to reorganize a Presbyterian congregation and subsequently a committed group started the John Sergeant Memorial Presbyterian Church. It is here that the Bible resurfaces under the care of tribal member Jamieson "Sote" Quinney, a member and elder of the Sergeant Memorial congregation. Quinney took the Bible to the Presbyterian Synod meeting in Milwaukee in 1917. Aware of his age, and not having anyone who wished to take responsibility for the Bible, Quinney had it placed in a safe in the church.[5] At some point prior to his death, however, and for reasons known only to him, Quinney brought the Bible into his home for safe keeping. Jamieson died in March of 1929, leaving the care of the Bible to his wife, Ella. At some time Reverend Frederick G. Westfall, pastor of the Sergeant Memorial Church, and not a tribal member, entered the Quinney home when Ella was away and took the Bible into his possession.

---

[4] Siemers, *Proud and Determined*, 174.
[5] Thelma Putnam, *Christian Religion Among the Stockbridge Munsee Band of Mohican Indians*, Arvid E. Miller Memorial Museum and Archives, Bowler, WI., 57, n.d.

The John Sergeant Memorial Presbyterian Church—2019

In 1929, Rev. Westfall began a correspondence with Mabel Choate (1870–1958), of Stockbridge, Massachusetts. Mabel was the daughter of wealthy New York lawyer, Joseph Hodges Choate (1832–1917), and had inherited the family's forty-four room "cottage," named Naumkeag, in Stockbridge. Mabel had purchased and moved John Sergeant's original house to a prominent location in Stockbridge with the intention of setting it up as a museum to the Mohican Indians and of Sergeant's mission among them. It was appropriately named the "Mission House."

At this point The Sergeant Memorial Church was in serious decline and no longer able to support Westfall's salary. In a letter to Choate, Westfall lamented the church's situation and realized it was in its last days. He writes "Times are changing here ... it is only a matter of time before the old John Sergeant Memorial Church will cease as an organization."[6] It may be that Westfall was genuinely concerned that Ayscough's Bible remain identified with the Mohicans, as he had rejected two offers from other ministers wanting to purchase it. The reason he finally decided to sell it to Choate may be inferred in her letter to him:

> I understand that the Indians are very poor, and have sold some of their papers and documents, to give them help during last year's winter months. If there is anything that I could do for them perhaps you could let me know. I should like to keep in touch with them through you; and if there are any documents or things of theirs which they would care to part with, I should be more than grateful if they would let me know. In doing so, I should like them to realize these things would remain permanently in the Mission House, surrounded by the associations of the past two hundred years.[7]

Whatever Rev. Westfall's motivation, the Bible was sold to Mable Choate in May of 1930 for $1000, and returned to its original home in Stockbridge. By 1937, the few remaining members of the Sergeant Memorial Church joined a Presbyterian Church in Gresham, and Sergeant Memorial closed its doors permanently. Today it serves as a storage building for a private residence. The Bible became all but forgotten by those in the tribe who knew of its existence.

Mabel Choate would turn over the Mission House and its artifacts to the Trustees of Reservations, a non-profit organization, founded in 1891, whose mandate is to preserve properties and lands of historical

---

[6] Siemers, *Proud and Determined*, 189–190.
[7] Siemers, *Proud and Determined*, 189.

significance in the Commonwealth of Massachusetts. Unknown to the tribe, the Bible was placed in a glass display case in the Mission House. There it remained for public viewing until a chance visit in 1951 by tribal member James Davids and family, who were from Wisconsin. In 1975, an earnest effort was begun on behalf of the Mohican tribe to repatriate their beloved Bible back to the reservation. Over the next fifteen years, an intense letter-writing and media campaign directed toward the Trustees was held, imploring them to return the Bible to its rightful owners. Much of the official correspondence from the tribe to the Trustees was ignored, and went unanswered. Finally, on April 19, 1990, and only with a threat of impending legal action, the Trustees signed a letter of agreement signifying their decision to return the Bible to the tribe, with some conditions surrounding its security. On March 11, 1991, ten members of the Mohican tribe retook possession of their sacred and beloved Bible. Siemers tells of the joyous return to the reservation:

> When the delegates were almost home, they contacted other members of the tribe and told them to meet them at a parking lot off highway 29 on the edge of Shawano. When the delegates arrived at the parking lot, they found over fifty people waiting for them, including members of a confirmation class that had made huge, colorful banners to celebrate the return of the Stockbridge Bible. ... They got back into their vehicles and formed a large convoy which headed back to the reservation, finally stopping at the Arvid E. Miller Memorial Museum where the Stockbridge Bible has been safely kept ever since.[8]

---

[8] Siemers, *Proud and Determined*, 221-222

4
JONATHAN EDWARDS

It was stated by Ezra Stiles (1727-1795), seventh president of Yale, that within thirty years of Jonathan Edwards' death, his works would pass into obscurity and that he would be all but forgotten.[1] He goes on to say that Edwards' works would be given, "transient notice perhaps scarce above oblivion," and that, "when posterity occasionally comes across them in the rubbish of libraries, the rare characters who may read and be pleased with them will be looked upon as singular and whimsical."[2] His predictions couldn't have been further from the truth. In fact, the works of Jonathan Edwards have consistently influenced theologians and Christian thought from the time he wrote them down to the present day. Indeed, Edwards remains one of the most studied of the eighteenth-century theologians.

Jonathan Edwards was totally devoted to the Word of God and the work of God in the heart of man. His great-grandson, Sereno E. Dwight, said that Edwards' "knowledge of the human heart and its operations, has scarcely been equaled by that of any uninspired preacher."[3] Dwight points to three reasons for Edwards' incredible perception regarding man's heart, and states them as "Edwards' perceptive reading of the

---

[1] Personal discussion with church historian Dr. Michael A.G. Haykin, Fellow of the Royal Historical Society. He stated that Stiles may either have gotten caught up in the Williams' hostility toward Edwards or that he believed Edwards' writings were too metaphysical, which was a frequent charge in the eighteenth and nineteenth centuries.

[2] Dane C. Ortlund, *Edwards on the Christian Life: Alive to the Beauty of God* (Wheaton, IL: Crossway, 2014), 15.

[3] Michael A.G. Haykin, *Jonathan Edwards The Holy Spirit In Revival* (Darlington, England: Evangelical Press, 2005), 2.

Scriptures; 'his thorough acquaintance with his own heart'; and his grasp of philosophy."[4] To that list I would also add Edwards' clear understanding of God's providential purpose in creation. John Piper says, "Edwards' answer to the question of why God created the world is this: to emanate the fullness of His Glory for His people to know, praise and enjoy."[5] As we shall see, Edwards was extremely well versed in his knowledge of Scripture and was completely dedicated to preaching the message of salvation and the glory of God. This short chronicle of the life of Edwards will discuss his spirituality as found in several of his most notable sermons, and conclude with an in-depth study of some of the sermons Edwards preached to the Mohicans while living in Stockbridge, Massachusetts.

Early Life and Education

Edwards was born in East Windsor, Connecticut on October 5, 1703. He was the fifth of eleven children and the only boy born to Rev. Timothy Edwards and Esther Stoddard Edwards.[6] The children were all over six feet tall and the locals around East Windsor would often jokingly refer to Timothy Edwards' "sixty feet of daughters!" Having four older and six younger sisters, Jonathan was no doubt under the strong influence of female perspectives in his life. While this may have given him a strong sensitivity to the needs of the lost in his ministry, his sense of scriptural truth came from the strict teaching of his father. Marsden tells us,

> Timothy Edwards ran a tight ship. Even if his wife Esther was practically in charge of household matters, we know from letters that Timothy wrote while briefly serving as a chaplain in the army that no domestic detail was too small to escape his oversight ("Let care be taken that the...barn door ben't left

---

[4] Haykin, *Jonathan Edwards*, 2.

[5] Owen Strachan and Doug Sweeney, *Jonathan Edwards, Lover of God* (Chicago, IL: Moody Publishers, 2010), 17.

[6] Strachan and Sweeney, *Jonathan Edwards*, 23.

open to the cattle"). He ran his church the same way, meticulously gauging the spiritual condition of any candidate to become a full communicant member and always expecting everyone to defer to proper authority.[7]

Jonathan's early education was at the hands of his father who, as Marsden says, "had the highest expectations for his only son. The attentive father was also an excellent teacher of Latin and Greek, both necessary languages for one desiring to enter college. Jonathan was a born student and his remarkable aptitudes must have gratified his father immensely."[8] We are told that,

> At an age when children today barely know the alphabet, Jonathan began the study of Latin under the tutelage of his father, who supplemented his pastoral income by tutoring boys preparing for college. Jonathan mastered Latin and progressed to Greek and Hebrew by age twelve.[9]

In September, 1716, Edwards, aged thirteen, entered Connecticut Collegiate School, later known as Yale University, in New Haven. He graduated first in his class in September of 1720 with a Bachelor's degree and went on to complete his Master's degree in 1722. His training in the spiritual aspects of life came predominantly from two sources: his father, Timothy, and his maternal grandfather, Solomon Stoddard, (1643 – 1729), who was "the most renowned man in the promising valley of the Connecticut River."[10] While Stoddard was a formidable Puritan presence in the life of his young grandson, the greater influence on his spiritual growth was his father. Marsden states:

---

[7] George M. Marsden, *A Short Life of Jonathan Edwards* (Grand Rapids: William B. Eerdmans Publishing Company, 2008), 15.
[8] Marsden, *A Short Life*, 16.
[9] Strachan and Sweeney, *Jonathan Edwards*, 25-26.
[10] George M. Marsden, *Jonathan Edwards A Life* (New Haven: Yale University Press, 2003), 11.

In his famous account of the "surprising Work of God" of 1734-35 in Northampton, Jonathan recorded that there had been "four or five" outpourings of the Spirit in "my honored father's parish, which has in times past been a place favored with mercies of this nature above any on this western side of New England, excepting Northampton." So, the father more directly than the grandfather set the footsteps in which Jonathan would try to follow.[11]

Conversion

Edwards' spiritual struggle with God began early and he frequently records his desire to live a pious life. Haykin recalls Edwards' confession from *Personal Narrative*:

> I had a variety of concerns and exercises about my soul from my childhood; but had two more remarkable seasons of awakening...The first time was when I was a boy, some years before I went to college, at a time of a remarkable awakening in my father's congregation...I used to pray five times a day in secret, and to spend much time in religious talk with other boys; and used to meet with them to pray together, and built a booth in a swamp, in a very retired spot, for a place of prayer... My affections seemed to be lively and easily moved, and I seemed to be in my element, when engaged in religious duties.[12]

But Edwards continued to fall back into his old habits, feeling the associated guilt of apostasy, though his deepest desire was to know God and his salvation fully within his soul. Salvation was to come to Edwards, however, probably around the spring of 1721. He writes in his *Personal Narrative*,

> The first instance that I remember of that sort of inward, sweet delight in God and divine things that I have lived much

---

[11] Marsden, *Jonathan Edwards*, 25.
[12] Haykin, *Jonathan Edwards*, 8.

in since, was on reading those words, I Tim. i:17. *Now unto the King eternal, immortal, invisible, the only wise God, be honour and glory for ever and ever, Amen.* As I read the words, there came into my soul, and was as it were diffused through it, a sense of the glory of the Divine Being; a new sense, quite different from any thing I ever experienced before. Never any words of scripture seemed to me as these words did. I thought with myself, how excellent a Being that was, and how happy I should be, if I might enjoy that God, and be rapt up to him in heaven, and be as it were swallowed up in him forever! I kept saying and as it were singing over these words of scripture to myself; and went to pray to God that I might enjoy him, and prayed in a manner quite different from what I used to do; with a new sort of affection.[13]

On his return home in the spring for vacation, he had a profound discussion with his father about his newfound faith. Marsden tells us,

Jonathan recalled that he was "pretty much affected" by this conversation, and when it ended, he walked alone into the fields for contemplation. "And as I was walking there," he reported, "and looked up on the sky and clouds; there came into my mind, a sweet sense of the glorious majesty and grace of God, that I know not how to express." ... "in a sweet conjunction; majesty and meekness joined together: it was a sweet and gentle, a holy majesty; and also, a majestic meekness; an awful sweetness; a high, and great, and holy gentleness."[14]

The change in Edwards was overwhelming. As he described the work of God in his life in his *Personal Narrative*, he repeatedly used the

---

[13] *Jonathan Edwards: Representative selections.* Ed. Clarence H. Faust and Thomas H. Johnson. (New York: American Book Company, 2002), http://mith.umd.edu/eada/html/display.php?docs=edwards_personalnarrative.xml&action=show.

[14] Marsden, *Jonathan Edwards*, 42.

word "sweet" to depict his new relationship with God. The Word of God became his meat and drink. Edwards said,

> From about that time, I began to have a new kind of apprehensions and ideas of Christ, and the work of redemption, and the glorious way of salvation by him. An inward, sweet sense of these things, at times, came into my heart; and my soul was led away in pleasant views and contemplations of them. And my mind was greatly engaged to spend my time in reading and meditating on Christ, on the beauty and excellency of his person, and the lovely way of salvation by free grace in him. I found no books so delightful to me, as those that treated of these subjects. Those words Cant. ii.1, used to be abundantly with me, *I am the Rose of Sharon, and the Lilly of the valleys*.[15]

Edwards in Love and in Ministry

Subsequent to his conversion in 1721, Edwards had a couple of small parish charges. After two relatively brief stints of pastoring—first to a small Scots Presbyterian congregation on William Street in New York[16] (August 1722-April 1723), and then at a Congregationalist church in Bolton, Connecticut (November 1723-May 1724)—Edwards moved back to his hometown of East Windsor.[17] After these pastorates, Edwards returned to Yale as a tutor for a couple of years and then, in August 1726, joined his grandfather, Solomon Stoddard, as his assistant in Northampton. Edwards was ordained on February 15, 1727 at the age of 23. Stoddard was 84.

In 1719 and during his years at Yale, Jonathan became acquainted with young Sarah Pierpont, daughter of James Pierpont, the minister of the First Congregationalist Church in New Haven, and a leader in the founding of Yale. Her great grandfather, Thomas Hooker, was founder

---

[15] Faust and Johnson, *Jonathan Edwards*, #4.
[16] M. X. Lesser, *Jonathan Edwards* (Boston, MA: Twayne Publishers, 1988), 4.
[17] Haykin, *Jonathan Edwards*, 10.

of Hartford. He was struck by Sarah's sense of the divine and her piety, even from an early age, and Haykin tells us that she was converted at age five.[18] To get a sense of the impact she had on Edwards; we must consult his personal testimony:

> They say there is a young lady in New Haven who is beloved of that almighty Being, who made and rules the world, and that there are certain seasons in which this great Being, in some way or other invisible, comes to her and fills her mind with exceeding sweet delight, and that she hardly cares for anything, except to meditate on him-that she expects after a while to be received up where he is, to be raised up out of the world and caught up into heaven; being assured that he loves her too well to let her remain from a distance from him always. There she is to dwell with him, and to be ravished with his love and delight forever. Therefore, if you present all the world before her, with the riches of its treasures, she disregards it and cares not for it, and is unmindful of any pain or affliction. She has a strange sweetness in her mind, and singular purity in her affections; is most just and conscientious in all her actions; and you could not persuade her to do anything wrong or sinful, if you would give her all the world, lest she should offend this great Being. She is of a wonderful sweetness, calmness and universal benevolence of mind; especially after those seasons in which this great God has manifested himself to her mind. She will sometimes go about from place to place, singing sweetly; and seems to be always of joy and pleasure; and no one knows for what. She loves to be alone, and to wander in the fields and on the mountains, and seems to have someone invisible always conversing with her.[19]

Edwards found a soul mate in Sarah, someone with whom he could not only share his earthly love, but his love of the heavenly Father as

---

[18] Haykin, *Jonathan Edwards*, 10.
[19] Strachan and Sweeney, *Jonathan Edwards*, 51-52.

well. They were married on July 28, 1727, and subsequently had eleven children, all of whom survived to adulthood, which was unprecedented for that period. Sarah was the perfect wife for Edwards as she diligently handled the affairs of the family, which allowed him the vital time he needed to devote to the ministry. As Stoddard's understudy, and also being newly married, the town council sought to ensure Edwards' essential needs were well cared for. Marsden notes:

> His marriage to Sarah in July, 1727 was a step signaling the young assistant's transition to adult and authoritative status. Under the leadership of Squire John Stoddard [Edwards' uncle], the town saw that the young couple were well settled as befit their status. As part of his initial settlement, Edwards was granted ten acres of land for a pasture and another forty acres farther from town that could be used for income. His annual salary was set with an inflation clause, probably reflecting advice from his father, who constantly fought with his town over his declining real income. The Northampton town meeting specifically agreed that "he should have an honourable and suitable maintenance according to the dignity of his office." In addition, he was given sufficient funds to purchase a home, so that shortly before his marriage he could acquire a "Mansion house, barn and home lot" of three acres on King Street near the church.[20]

As Stoddard's heir and assistant in the pulpit, Edwards was getting lots of practice preaching and was under the strong influence of Stoddard's doctrinal teachings, especially regarding church membership and the Lord's Supper. Stoddard's own belief was that the Lord's Supper could be used as a means to bring people to salvation:

> In Northampton he (Stoddard) broadened the standards for full church membership to all adults who professed the doctrines of the church, submitted to its discipline, and promised to attempt to live morally. Such broader standards meant that

---

[20] Marsden, *Jonathan Edwards*, 123-124.

most if not all upright citizens of the community were likely to become full members of the church...Stoddard also accepted a broader standard for baptism, one that was already being adopted in many New England towns by the time of his entry into the ministry in the 1670s. Called the "half-way covenant," this policy provided that even if adults, who had been baptized as children, did not become communicant members, their children could be baptized.[21]

While Edwards outwardly seemed to accept his grandfather's stand as it related to the church and membership, inwardly he struggled. The question which plagued Edwards was that if the communion table were open to all, how would it be possible to discern those of real faith? Marsden tells us, "During the years he spent under Stoddard's tutelage, Jonathan was reading or rereading his grandfather's works and wrestling with whether it was possible to devise a science of identifying visible saints."[22] This caused Jonathan great stress in his work with Stoddard and no doubt they debated it at length, possibly agreeing to disagree on the matter. That he disagreed with his grandfather on this point can be attributed to the foundational teaching he had, and continued to receive, from his father Timothy. Marsden notes that, "In these early days Jonathan's internal anxieties must have been great because, among other things, Timothy Edwards was not so far away—especially not from his son's psyche. Jonathan, despite his creativity, remained remarkably close to his father's opinions on most issues."[23] This issue would bring Edwards to a crisis later on in his ministry.

Edwards Succeeds Stoddard

Solomon Stoddard died on February 11, 1729,[24] thus leaving Edwards in charge of the Northampton congregation. It is a matter of history that

---

[21] Marsden, *A Short Life*, 36-37.
[22] Marsden, *Jonathan Edwards*, 122.
[23] Marsden, *Jonathan Edwards*, 123.
[24] Lesser, *Jonathan Edwards*, 8.

during Stoddard's tenure, though there had been periods of small revival within the congregation, there had been nothing of note since 1718. Edwards was disturbed by the lack of spirituality within the congregation and the worldliness that had especially been affecting the younger people in the area. He notes,

> Just after my grandfather's death, it seemed to be a time of extraordinary dullness in religion: licentiousness for some years prevailed among the youth of the town; they were many of them very much addicted to night-walking, and frequenting the tavern, and lewd practices, wherein some by their example, exceedingly corrupted others.[25]

Subsequent to Stoddard's death, Edwards, who had always been somewhat of a frail man, suffered a couple of severe bouts of illness wherein he had to vacate the pulpit for a period of time to recuperate. Much of this illness may have been brought on by the stress of overwork and of trying to live up to the demanding standards of his congregation. In the 1730s, however, as Edwards preached a series of sermons on justification by faith, the Spirit of God began to work in the hearts of the people and a new revival began. Edwards felt there was a direct link between the solid preaching of God's Word and the moving of the Spirit in the hearts of the hearers. Haykin states, "It was the exposition of this central feature of the New Testament that Edwards saw as the major catalyst that the Holy Spirit used to begin an extraordinary revival in Northampton."[26] People began to exhibit changed lives and the revival spread throughout the Connecticut Valley.

In November of 1736 Edwards recorded this amazing work of God in a work entitled, *A Faithful Narrative of a Surprising Work of God,* which he sent to Rev. Benjamin Colman (1673-1747) in Boston. The Puritan thought on conversion had been that it was a multistep process, typically taking a number of years. Edwards' observation and argument

---

[25] Haykin, *Jonathan Edwards*, 14.
[26] Haykin, *Jonathan Edwards*, 15.

from his experience in Northampton, however, was that the Holy Spirit could accomplish salvation in an individual instantly. He states that, "Conversion is a great and glorious work of God's power, at once changing the heart, and infusing life into the dead soul; though the grace then implanted more gradually displays itself in some than in others."[27]

The revival of 1734–1735 came to an abrupt halt on June 1, 1736, when Edwards' uncle, Joseph Hawley, concluded that the only assurance of salvation was to be in God's presence, and committed suicide by cutting his throat. Hawley was well-known in Northampton as he was not only a successful merchant, but had been the town's clerk since 1716. The news of his death reverberated throughout the community and Edwards in particular was affected, not only because Hawley was his kin, but because he was Hawley's pastor. In a postscript to his letter to Colman, Edwards explained that Hawley had a genetic disposition to depression and melancholy; his mother having succumbed to depression years earlier. He stated that the revival had caused Hawley to be more concerned for his soul and he could not sleep since he was preoccupied with his lost condition before God. Marden concludes, "Much weakened by loss of sleep, Hawley would no longer listen to reason or take advice."[28] Becoming increasingly more agitated and despondent, he chose the only path that would give him mental and emotional rest. Edwards concluded that this was the outworking of Satan who was fighting against the revival with great vigor. He stated to Colman, "Satan seems to be in a great rage, at this extraordinary breaking forth of the work of God. I hope it is because he knows that he has but a short time."[29]

---

[27] Jonathan Edwards, *A Faithful Narrative of the Surprising Work of God.*, http://www.jonathan-edwards.org/Narrative.html (Accessed February 13, 2018).

[28] Marden, *Jonathan Edwards*, 164.

[29] C. C. Goen, ed., *The Works of Jonathan Edwards* (New Haven: Yale University Press, 1992), 4:206.

Another great revival swept the colonies in 1740–1742, in conjunction with the Great Awakening that had begun in England under the preaching of George Whitefield and the Wesley brothers. Whitefield was a powerful preacher in the Church of England; when the pulpits of the churches became closed to him because of his forceful and almost theatrical preaching style, however, he began to conduct outdoor services. Whitefield came to Boston on September 18, 1740 and visited with Edwards and his family in October of 1740, later reporting that during his preaching, "Mr. Edwards wept during the whole time of the exercise."[30] Edwards himself stated that "the congregation was extraordinarily melted by each sermon, almost the whole assembly being in tears for a great part of the time."[31] We can only speculate as to the cause of the emotional reaction of Edwards to Whitefield's preaching—perhaps it was the result of seeing so many people being moved by the Holy Spirit, or perhaps from the Spirit working in Edwards himself, who no doubt longed for such deep teaching.

Whitefield preached five times while in Northampton and it may have been during these services that some of Edwards' own children were saved. In a later letter written to Whitefield in December, Edwards spoke specifically of the great impact the preaching had on the young people. McDermott tells us that in the letter, "He noted of special importance 'a considerable number of our young people, some of them children, having already been savingly brought home to Christ. Among these young converts was one, if not more, of my children.'"[32] Whitefield, still unmarried, was very impressed with the Edwards family and wrote in his journal:

---

[30] Arnold A. Dallimore, *George Whitefield: The Life and Times of the Great Evangelist of the Eighteenth Century Revival* (Westchester, Il: Cornerstone Books, 1980), 1:539.

[31] Letter of Jonathan Edwards to the Reverend Thomas Prince, dated December 12, 1743. George S. Claghorn, ed., *The Works of Jonathan Edwards* (New Haven: Yale University Press, 1992), 16:116.

[32] Harry S. Stout, "Edwards and Revival" in *Understanding Jonathan Edwards*, ed. Gerald R. McDermott (Oxford: Oxford University Press, 2009), 46.

Felt great satisfaction in being at the house of Mr. Edwards. A sweeter couple I have not yet seen. Their children were not dressed in silks and satins, but plain, as become the children of those, who, in all things, ought to be the examples of Christian simplicity. Mrs. Edwards is adorned with a meek and quiet spirit; she talked solidly of the things of God, and seemed to be such a helpmeet for her husband, that she caused me to renew those prayers which, for some months, I have put up to God, that He would be pleased to send me a daughter of Abraham to be my wife.[33]

It would seem Whitefield's prayers were answered, as he married Elizabeth James on November 14, 1741 at Capel Martin, Caerphilly, Wales.[34]

The new revival that swept the area met with considerable resistance from Rev. Charles Chauncy (1705-1787), who was vehemently opposed to it, and especially the more fantastic evidences of the Spirit. Further discredit to the movement came from the likes of James Davenport (1716-1757), who became wildly fanatical not only in his preaching, but in his behavior. In an attempt to bring balance among all involved, Edwards published two treatises. Haykin states,

> Edwards had produced a couple of works that sought to find a middle ground between "pious zealots," such as Davenport, and "cold, diabolical opposers," such as Chauncy: *The Distinguishing Marks of a Work of the Spirit of God* (1741) and *Some Thoughts concerning the present Revival of Religion in New England* (1742).[35]

---

[33] *George Whitefield's Journals* (London: The Banner of Truth Trust, 1960), 476-477.
[34] *The Life of George Whitefield*, https://banneroftruth.org/us/resources/articles/2015/life-george-whitefield/ (accessed February 17, 2018).
[35] Haykin, *Jonathan Edwards*, 20.

He argued diligently from Scripture that the revival that was bringing about repentance was truly an outworking of God's Holy Spirit and not merely the emotional reaction of people to dynamic speakers.

Unfortunately, it appeared that the new outpouring of God's Spirit on the people of New England was not to last. Edwards lamented in letter to his Scottish friend, Reverend William McCullough on March 5, 1744 that, "Tis probable that you have been informed by other correspondents before now what the present state of things in New England is. It is indeed on many accounts very melancholy."[36] Edwards was truly upset that the people had slipped into a condition of spiritual dryness and put it down to two causes. First, the people, in neglecting their spiritual needs, had given way to Satan, "And through want of watchfulness and sensibleness of the danger and temptation that there is in such circumstances, many were greatly exposed. And the devil taking the advantage, multitudes were soon, and to themselves insensibly, led far away from God and their duty."[37] This led Edwards to the second cause of their spiritual dullness: God was upset with them and hence had withdrawn his Spirit. Claghorn quotes Edwards, who said, "God was provoked that he was not sanctified in this height of advancement, as he ought to have been. He saw our spiritual pride and self-confidence, and the polluted flames that arose of intemperate, unhallowed zeal; and he soon in a great measure withdrew from us."[38] This pride, Edwards noted, resulted in a downhill slide, with the result that "the enemy has come in like a flood." What is noteworthy in the wording of Edwards' letter is that in using "we" and "us" he is not casting the blame solely on his congregation but fully accepts the responsibility as their pastor, and shares the offence. Despite his fervent efforts and solid Biblical teaching, Edwards' ministry would hit a dead end in Northampton in 1744.

---

[36] Claghorn, *The Works*, 16:134.
[37] Claghorn, *The Works*, 16:134.
[38] Claghorn, *The Works*, 16:134.

Dismissal from the Northampton Pulpit

There were three primary causes of Edwards' dismissal from the Northampton pulpit. One was a dispute regarding the congregation's failure to adequately cover his salary; the second was Edwards' handling of an issue related to the youth; and the final, most crucial, contention was how he chose to deal with Stoddard's half-way covenant.

The spiritual dearth among the people, especially the youth, led to the first major event in the demise of his ministry in Northampton and involved what became known as the "Young Folks' Bible," or the "Bad Book." Johnson mentions that it was not surprising that there were problems of a moral nature following quickly on the heels of a revival, "Periods of moral laxity followed hard upon the emotional strain of revivals, and such a period of laxity was due in Northampton in the early forties."[39] It came to Edwards' attention that some of the young men in his church had been circulating medical books on midwifery and had taken to talking lewdly among themselves as well as making rude and suggestive comments to some of the young girls of the church, particularly about their monthly cycle. Edwards, feeling it was his duty as the pastor to get to the truth, sent a letter dated August, 1744 to Eleazar Hannam's wife. He wrote:

> It has been testified by one befo[re the][40] Church, that she was once at the [John (or) Moll] Macklin's House, where were Oli[ver War]ner, and Medad Lyman reading [a book] about women kind, that which wa[s very] unclean to be read; and that they [made] sport of what they read before some[e wo]men kind; and that Thankfull Parso[ns said] you were

---

[39] Thomas H. Johnson, "Jonathan Edwards and the 'Young Folks' Bible." *The New England Quarterly.* 5, no.1 (Jan., 1932). https://www.jstor.org/stable/359489?read-now=1&refreqid=excelsior%3Aeb85a5623ac10ba48cf820074d6dd6be&seq=12#page_scan_tab_contents (accessed June 26, 2019).

[40] Brackets contain letters and words presumed to be in the manuscript since it was trimmed along an edge to fit Edwards' sermon book. Some punctuation added for ease of reading.

there. This therefore is [to de]sire you, as you are a member of th[e Chris]tian Church, and would maintain [Com]munion of Churches, whereby they [are ob]liged to assist one another as occai[sion arises] to send an exact and full Testimony [of all] that you know relating to this ma[tter] particularly as near as you can, how [unclean(?)] it was, which of these two young [men] read in the Book, whether one or [both] of them, what the Book was abo[ut,] whether it was about women's having childre[n,] whether they seem'd to make sport [and di]version of what was read, whether [they] took occasion from it to run upon the [girls] and the like. In thus giving [this] Testimony I think you will do wha[t you] are obliged to do as a Christian.[41]

Edwards collected information related to the matter and, after preaching a sermon on Hebrews 12:15–16, told the men of the church to remain behind to discuss the issue. A committee was chosen to hear the proceedings. It was here that Edwards made a serious error in judgment that would forever polarize the community against him. After pronouncing a time that they would meet at his home, Edwards proceeded to read out a list of those requested to be present for questioning, but in his proclamation, he failed to distinguish the witnesses from the accused. Marsden tells us,

> Some of the young people named were from, or related to, prominent families. According to [Samuel] Hopkins, before the townspeople reached their homes some leading citizens were condemning the procedure. By the time the committee met "the town was suddenly all on a blaze."[42]

The committee met and testimonies related to the accusations were taken down. The attestant's name was recorded, and the details of the

---

[41] Johnson, "Jonathan Edwards," 41.
[42] Marsden, *Jonathan Edwards*, 293.

evidence given. A couple of examples as compiled by Johnson will be sufficient to show the nature of the infractions.

> Bathsheba.[43] At David Burns. Noah Baker, Timothy Root and Elkanah Burt reading in a Book that they called the Bible in a Laughing way. all read in Tim Root read most,—(about the time that Noah Baker was married) read it before Her. Naomi [Mather(?)]. Laugh ready to kill them and catch hold of the girls and shook 'em. Tim Root in particular called it young folks Bible. the Book was exceeding unclean to the top of Baseness. The Book which they read was about women. Samuell Burts Book they said. it about women's Having children. Had seen the Book at Sam. Burts once before[44]

> John Lancton a fortnight ago last Friday was at the farm where I was and was talking of such things and he boasted that he had Read Aristotle. he talked about his reading the Book more than once talked about the things that was in that Book in a most unclean manner a long time. Betty Jenks and Moll Waters there. he spoke of the Book as a Granny Book. When I checked him he Laughed and he talked exceeding uncleanly. And Lasciviously so that I never heard any fellow Go so far. After he was gone we the young women that were there agreed that we never heard any such talk come out of any man[']s mouth whatsoever. It seem'd to me to be almost as bad as tongue could express.[45]

It seems that while the depositions were being taken, those who had been summoned and accused became rude and belligerent toward Edwards, the committee, and the proceedings. The committee meeting notes recorded:

---

[43] Bathsheba Negro was a slave girl of Major Seth Pomeroy.

[44] Johnson, *Jonathan Edwards*, 45. Some punctuation added for ease of reading.

[45] Johnson, *Jonathan Edwards*, 47. Some punctuation added for ease of reading.

> Moses Hannam testifies that while the Committee of this Church were sitting the first time at the Pastor's House, Timothy Root moved to other to go away, and said to 'em in the Presence of a Considerable number of Persons come we'll go away; do you think I'll be kept here for nothing? And speaking of the Committee said they are nothing but men molded up of a little Dirt. I don't care a Turd, or I don't care a Fart for any of them.[46]

In the end the Committee was satisfied that it had completed its work and the ringleaders were identified as Oliver Warner and Timothy and Simeon Root. Marsden tells us

> Three young men—Oliver Warner, an enterprising apprentice who had offered to show the principal book to others for ten shillings, and cousins Timothy and Simeon Root—were the leading offenders, but up to twenty of the most unmarried young men had been peripherally involved. All but three were church members.[47]

It was deemed that they would make a public confession of their transgressions and Edwards prepared the confessions, "in which they 'publickly' acknowledged and asked pardon for their 'scandalous contemptuous Behaviour towards the authority of this Church,'" dated June 3, 1744.[48] Warner's confession was as follows:

> Whereas Two Persons viz. Joanna Clark and Bathsheba Maj. Pumroy's Servant, have testified that they heard me utter certain very unclean and Lascivious Expressions, in what I said to them some time last year, altho' I do not remember my using those Expressions, yet because I might use them or some other unclean Expressions like them, and forget it in so

---

[46] Johnson, *Jonathan Edwards*, 50–51.
[47] Marsden, *Jonathan Edwards*, 293.
[48] Johnson, *Jonathan Edwards*, 51.

long a time, and inasmuch as they do both of them so positively and constantly declare that I did utter those expressions, I do therefore give them credit, and suspect myself; and accordingly do now appear publickly to humble myself for that which is so unbecoming of a Christian, and of a very scandalous nature; and ask forgiveness of God and his People, and promise to be more watchfull for the future to avoid all Lascivious, vain and Light conversation, and in both word and deed to behave myself with that sobriety and Purity that becomes the Gospel.[49]

Edwards was vexed by this problem for a number of good reasons. These young men, in their twenties, were his spiritual children and congregants. Many of them had, just a few years previously, made strong confessions during the period of revival. Indeed, in March of 1742 many of them subscribed to a covenantal document that Edwards had prepared. In a letter to the Reverend Thomas Prince, Edwards outlines the covenant in full, and it seems that one of the key elements it articulated had been directly violated as a result of the recent moral issue. It said,

And furthermore we promise that we will strictly avoid all freedoms and familiarities in company, so tending either to stir up or gratify a lust of lasciviousness, that we cannot in our consciences think will be approved by the infinitely pure and holy eye of God.[50]

Though Edwards was not ignorant of the fact that young men were especially prone to the temptations of the flesh, their flagrant, disgusting, and frankly despicable behavior towards women was, for him, a serious violation. This infraction also bothered him as a father because his own young daughters had also been taunted by these men and subjected to their rude language. One further thing that disturbed Edwards was

---

[49] Johnson, *Jonathan Edwards*, 51–52.
[50] Claghorn, *Works*, 124.

the serious hypocrisy demonstrated by these young men who, while blatantly indulging in acts they knew to be sinful, would then come to communion on Sunday. Edwards had preached several sermons related to the improper coming to the Lord's Table which were directed primarily at those in the congregation who still held to his grandfather Stoddard's half-way covenant. Edwards firmly believed that approaching the communion table in an unworthy manner was to openly mock the death of Christ and to bring judgment upon oneself. While the perpetrators ultimately were dealt with, the townsfolk were very upset with how Edwards had handled it and serious discontent among the townspeople ensued.

Edwards himself was also becoming increasingly disturbed by the half-way covenant and finally, in December of 1748, declared to his congregation that only professing believers were allowed to come to the Lord's Table for communion. This stand precipitated a major uprising within the church; leading the charge against Edwards were his own cousins, the Williams family. The conflict continued to fester and divide not only the congregation but also the local community. For his part, Edwards sought to educate everyone from Scripture on the proper mode of administering the Lord's Supper and ensuring those who took it were in a right standing with God. Marsden recounts how it all came to a head:

> Finally, in February he took matters into his own hands and announced a series of five Thursday lectures on the topic. Predictably, few of his congregation attended, although people from neighboring communities filled up the audience. Edwards scheduled the first lecture for February 15, the day the county courts were meeting in the town. His cousin Israel Williams was particularly furious at this maneuver and at the Court of Common Pleas for adjourning to hear the lectures. The Court of General Session of the Peace, on which Colonel Williams himself sat, refused to adjourn, and Williams made several vehement speeches against his cousin, calling him a

"tyrant" who was "unsufferable" in "lording it over [his] people."[51]

Marsden tells us:

> Finally, the matter was settled by calling in a council of clergy and laymen from ten surrounding churches. When the council polled church members, only twenty-three of the 230 men who voted supported Edwards. The visiting council was already divided along partisan lines, and on a close vote they agreed with the town majority to immediately dismiss Edwards from his pastorate.[52]

Edwards may have misjudged the timing of this new resolution to only serve communion to baptized members, but felt in his heart that he could convince the congregation with arguments from the Bible. Marsden articulates the main reason for Edwards' failure as follows,

> As he himself later recognized, he also did not take sufficiently into account the degree to which many of the townspeople viewed the great Solomon Stoddard almost as a deity—and that they accordingly regarded a defence of Stoddard's views as a matter of high religious duty.[53]

Indeed, many had referred to Stoddard as "the Pope of the Connecticut Valley." As Edwards continued to be harassed by conflicts and false accusations, the local townsfolk, at their own expense, even commissioned a treatise entitled, *The True State of the Question Concerning the Qualifications Necessary to Lawful Communion in the Christian Sacraments*. It was authored by Edwards' cousin, Solomon Williams, and by all accounts was not very well written.

Not surprisingly, Edwards felt he had been grossly misunderstood and misrepresented in this work and set to rebutting Williams in a

---

[51] Marsden, *Jonathan Edwards*, 359.
[52] Marsden, *A Short Life*, 113.
[53] Marsden, *A Short Life*, 114.

lengthy response.[54] His antagonists, however, sought a more gifted writer to respond to anything Edwards might produce in the future, and settled on another one of Edwards' cousins, Elisha Williams. He had been Rector of Yale but after leaving became involved in local politics and business. As it turned out, possibly due to an impending trip to England, Elisha was unable to complete a response to Edwards, but turned his notes over to his brother Solomon. Solomon proved unequal to the task, and Edwards systematically dismantled his rhetoric in a paper he published in 1752 entitled *Misrepresentations Corrected, and Truth Vindicated*. Marsden states, "Solomon Williams in his answer to Edwards made the mistake of overstating his case, thus setting himself up for his logician cousin, who proceeded to chop his arguments into splinters."[55] What these events show is that the ghost of Solomon Stoddard remained in the church at Northampton through his progeny among the Williams family. Edwards may have felt that he would get a reprieve from this troublesome branch of the family when he left Northampton but, as we shall see, this was not to be the case.

Besides the theological disputes Edwards was experiencing with the Northampton congregation, there was also the issue of his salary. The Edwards family was increasingly feeling financial pressures in the midst of a growing family as his salary was not covering inflationary costs. The town was also behind on its payments to him, and Marsden states,

> Edwards' salary, while relatively generous, was not keeping up with the combination of rising prices and a growing family. Also, since money was scarce, payments were often slow. In March 1744, Sarah, who managed the family finances, asked the town for past-due salary, stating that "Mr. Edwards is under such obligation that he can't possibly do without it."[56]

---

[54] David D. Hall, ed., *The Works of Jonathan Edwards* (New Haven: Yale University Press, 1994), 12:365.
[55] Marsden, *A Life*, 367–368.
[56] Marsden, *Jonathan Edwards*, 301–302.

To further make the Edwards' family life difficult, the town removed his access to the property he had been given to pasture his animals. Edwards argued that he had been granted the use of the property, but his plea fell on deaf ears.[57] The Edwards family stayed in Northampton for a further year while Jonathan looked for another charge. Ironically, the church found it necessary to call on him several times to preach the service when no pastor was available to them.

Edwards did some serious thinking and praying about his future work for God. He turned down an offer to go to Scotland, possibly because he felt inadequate to take on another sizeable charge in the wake of his apparent failure in Northampton. He preached his *A Farewell Sermon Preached at the First Precinct in Northampton, After the People's Public Rejection of Their Minister* on June 22, 1750 and in it warned the congregation about the false logic and doctrinal statements contained in Williams' book. He told them that if some of the arguments were followed to their logical conclusion, they would lead directly to Arminianism. He also cautioned them against ideologies "which have lately appeared in Northampton that tend to lead the young people among you apace into a liking to the new, fashionable, lax schemes of divinity, which have so greatly prevailed in New England as of late."[58] Despite the vehement attacks on his person and the efforts to ruin him as a minister, Edwards maintained his calm and decorum throughout the whole time, and those who supported him through the ordeal saw his true godly spirit shine forth. We find recorded in the diary of Reverend David Hall the following testimonial,

> I never saw the least symptoms in his countenance ... but he appeared like a man of God, whose happiness was out of the reach of his enemies, and whose treasure was not only a future but a present good, overbalancing all imaginable ills of

---

[57] Marsden, *Jonathan Edwards*, 363.
[58] Hall, *The Works*, 12:502.

life, even to the astonishment of many, who could not be at rest without his dismission.[59]

Haykin explains:

> The reasons for such calmness were at least twofold. The God whom Edwards loved and adored was a sovereign ruler in all human affairs, and what had taken place between him and his congregation ultimately came from the hand of a sovereign and omni-benevolent God. ... Second, Edwards genuinely loved his people, and despite what had happened, he was determined not to be embittered towards them.[60]

After a three-month trial period, in the summer of 1751 he accepted the charge to the Mohican Indian mission town of Stockbridge, Massachusetts, replacing John Sergeant, and moved his family there from Northampton in August. Frazier states, "To the Indian flock he was just a new shepherd. But to some of his Massachusetts contemporaries, he was an eccentric, outdated clergyman."[61] Initially it seemed that a move to a remote and sparsely inhabited area, to a people who had no preconceived notions about him, would be a good move for Edwards. This was not to be the case, however, as Abigail Sergeant, John Sergeant's widow, and daughter of Ephraim Williams, opposed Edwards replacing her husband as minister to the Stockbridge Mohicans. The Williams clan, heavily influenced by Ephraim and Abigail, already had what they considered an ideal new man in the person of Ezra Stiles. It may be that Abigail, who was still only twenty-seven, saw Stiles not

---

[59] Ola Elizabeth Winslow, *Jonathan Edwards, 1703-1758: A Biography* (New York: McMillan Co., 1940), 256.

[60] Haykin, *Jonathan Edwards*, 24.

[61] Patrick Frazier, *The Mohicans of Stockbridge* (Lincoln: University of Nebraska Press, 1992), 90.

only as a ministerial replacement to the people but also a suitable candidate for a new husband.[62] Stiles came for a week and preached on the two Sundays, staying at Abigail's home. However, Stiles was going through a time of spiritual indecision, seriously questioning his faith and ultimately landing on Deism as a belief. Marsden states that in a letter Stiles had told Abigail that he had "no other religion but that of *Nature* and the *Bible*," and even had misgivings about the Bible![63] Stiles withdrew as a candidate on the advice of his father, Reverend Isaac Stiles, who, ironically, had been mentored by Edwards in college.

Edwards in Stockbridge

It was a time of emotional upheaval and turmoil for the Edwards' family as some of his daughters were married and there was an ever-present threat due to the French and Indian War. The French had recruited the Indians in Canada to join them in the battle against the British, and they had taken to raiding colonies in New England. The raiding parties were unbelievably brutal to any settlers they came upon in their raids. But in all this uncertainty the family continually trusted in God's providence and, four days after preaching his farewell sermon to his congregation in Northampton, Edwards wrote to John Erskine, a dear and trusted Christian brother, in Scotland, stating,

> We are in the hands of God, and I bless him. I am not anxious concerning his disposal of us. I hope I shall not distrust him, nor be unwilling to submit to his will. And I have cause of thankfulness, that there seems also to be such a disposition in my family.[64]

---

[62] A complete discussion of this topic can be found in "Abigail," Chapter 5, Edmund S. Morgan, *The Gentle Puritan: A Life of Ezra Stiles, 1727-1795* (New York: W. W. Norton & Company. Inc., 1962).

[63] Marsden, *Jonathan Edwards*, 379.

[64] George S. Claghorn, ed., *The Works of Jonathan Edwards* (New Haven: Yale University Press, 1992), 16:355.

Edwards would also write to another friend, "What will become of us, God only knows."[65] What is certain is that Edwards considered this calling as an opportunity to evangelize the Indians.

While many theologians dispute that Edwards was mission-minded, Marsden states, "For Edwards the preeminent goal was to reach the Indians with the gospel."[66] It is important to note that Edwards had been closely involved in David Brainerd's mission to the Indians. In fact, just three years prior to them going to Stockbridge Brainerd himself had spent the remaining days of his life with the Edwards family and died in their Northampton home. It can be speculated with some confidence that they had many discussions regarding the evangelizing of the Indians and that this profoundly affected Edwards. In *An Account of the Life of the late Reverend Mr. David Brainerd,* Edwards would write,

> And if we consider the degree and manner in which he from time to time, sought and hoped for an extensive work of grace among them, I think, we have reason to hope, that the wonderful things, which God wrought among them by him, are but a forerunner of something yet much more glorious and extensive of that kind; and this may justly be an encouragement, to well-disposed charitable persons, to "honour the Lord with their substance, by contributing, as they are able, to promote the spreading of the gospel among them."[67]

Edwards' missions-mindedness, however, had been a part of his focus from very early on in his Christian life. In his *Personal Narrative,* recounting his life shortly after becoming a believer. Edwards clearly states,

---

[65] Marsden, *A Short Life,* 126.

[66] Marsden, *Jonathan Edwards,* 408-409.

[67] Jonathan Edwards, *An Account of the Life of the late Reverend Mr. David Brainerd* (Edinburgh: John Gray and Gayin Alston, 1765), 311.

> I had great longings for the advancement of Christ's kingdom in the world. My secret prayer used to be in great part taken up in praying for it. If I heard the least hint of anything that happened in any part of the world, that appeared to me, in some respect or other, to have a favorable aspect on the interest of Christ's kingdom, my soul eagerly catched at it; and it would much animate and refresh me ... I very frequently used to retire into a solitary place, on the banks of Hudson's River, at some distance from the city, for contemplation on divine things, and secret converse with God; and had many sweet hours there. Sometimes Mr. Smith and I walked there together, to converse of the things of God; and our conversation used much to turn on the advancement of Christ's kingdom in the world, and the glorious things that God would accomplish for his church in the latter days.[68]

There can be no doubt that Edwards was fully committed to preaching the gospel to everyone who would hear the message of salvation, and it was his desire to have the gospel preached throughout the world. Later in *Personal Narrative* he would again reflect,

> My heart has been much on the advancement of Christ's kingdom in the world. The histories of the past advancement of Christ's kingdom, have been sweet to me. When I have read histories of past ages, the pleasantest thing in all my reading has been, to read of the kingdom of Christ being promoted ... and my mind has been much entertained and delighted, with the Scripture promises and prophecies, of the future glorious advancement of Christ's kingdom on earth.[69]

As we shall discover in the content of his sermons to his Indian charges, he was very much concerned for the condition of their souls and sought diligently, in the easiest and simplest of terms, to bring to them the gospel of salvation in Christ. What is particularly noteworthy of Edwards'

---

[68] Claghorn, *The Works*, 16:797.
[69] Claghorn, *The Works*, 16:800.

time in Stockbridge is that, away from the controversy that had plagued him in Northampton, he now had the opportunity to write his major theological works, recounting God's goodness, grace and the power of the Holy Spirit in the life of the believer. Haykin concurs as he says,

> The usual account of his time at Stockbridge from 1751 to early 1758 concentrates on Edwards' literary achievements. And this is not surprising, for it was during these years that Edwards wrote those books that established him as the "greatest theologian of the eighteenth century."[70]

Marden also states, "In Stockbridge, in addition to his preaching and pastoral duties, he produced four major treatises, two of which are often regarded as classics in the history of Christianity and in the history of American intellectual life."[71] The four works were *Freedom of the Will* (1754), *Original Sin* (1758), and *Two Dissertations*, which were published in 1765, after his death. In his noteworthy Stockbridge work *A Careful and Strict Enquiry into the Modern Prevailing Notions of that Freedom of Will, Which is Supposed to be Essential to Moral Agency, Virtue and Vice, Reward and Punishment, Praise and Blame* completed in 1753 and published in 1754, Edwards makes a clear and concise defense of Calvinism. Edwards' other notable works *End for Which God Created the World*, and *True Virtue* were combined into *Two Dissertations*. In this treatise Edwards addresses the idea circulating in his day that God created the world only for man's pleasure and happiness. Edwards argues that the happiness of humanity was not God's primary reason for creation, but rather his own glory and magnification, demonstrated to his creation through his attributes.

As mentioned previously, the hamlet of Stockbridge had been established in 1734 as a settlement of Indians and a number of white New England families. The original design was to integrate the two societies,

---

[70] Haykin, *Jonathan Edwards*, 25.
[71] Marden, *Jonathan Edwards*, 389.

with the ultimate goal of "civilizing the savages by making them Christian." This was to be primarily accomplished by setting up permanent dwelling structures and teaching the native Indians animal husbandry and farming techniques, as a way of self-sustenance. Additionally, a school was built in the community to teach the Indian boys English, literature, and religion. When Edwards arrived in June of 1751, he found 250 Mohicans, 42 Mohawks of the Six Nations, and a dozen or so New England families which had volunteered to move.[72] Leading the group of New Englanders was Colonel Ephraim Williams, a member of the family that had caused Edwards so much grief back in Northampton. Williams, besides being a soldier, was a determined land investor. As has been stated, Edwards was replacing John Sergeant, who was married to Abigail Williams, Ephraim's daughter. Captain Ephraim Williams Jr., Abigail's half-brother, vehemently opposed Edwards' appointment to Stockbridge, and when they resigned themselves to the fact that he would be coming, Ephraim's response was that the only good that would come from Edwards' appointment would be to "raise the price of my land."[73] "Sarah Cabot Sedgwick and Christina Sedgwick Marquand note of Abigail Williams that, 'The Mission with her; as with her father; was the means to the end of developing the town of Stockbridge, and with it the fortunes of the Williams family.'"[74] Captain Ephraim Williams Jr. also did all he could to oppose Edwards' appointment to the Stockbridge mission. Marsden states:

> In May 1751 he wrote to his cousin by marriage, the Reverend Jonathan Ashley of Deerfield, enumerating the reasons he had opposed Edwards. First, "he was not sociable" and so (quoting Scripture) "not apt to teach," Second, 'he was a

---

[72] Stephen J. Nichols, "Last of the Mohican Missionaries," in *The Legacy of Jonathan Edwards*, D. G. Hart, Sean Michael Lucas, and, Stephen J, Nichols, eds. (Grand Rapids, MI: Baker, 2003), 48.

[73] Colonel Ephraim Williams to Ephraim Williams Jr., 2 May 1751, cited in Wyllis E. Wright, *Colonel Ephraim Williams: A Documentary Life* (Pittsfield, MA.: Berkshire County Historical Society, 1970), 61.

[74] Nichols, "Last of the Mohican Missionaries," 49.

very great bigot, for he would not admit any person into heaven, but those that agreed fully to his sentiment, a doctrine deeply tinged with that of the Romish church." ... Third, he was too old to learn the Indians' tongue. Fourth, the military man could neither understand nor agree to Edwards' principles on the sacraments and, he wrote, "that I had heard almost every gentleman in the country say the same."[75]

Knowing that he was going from "the frying pan into the fire," so to speak, why would Edwards decide to go to Stockbridge anyway? On top of his previously noted desire for missions, it turns out that he already had a connection to the Stockbridge community. As Nichols tells us,

> Additionally, Edwards had a long-standing interest in Indian missions, beginning in the mid-1730s. He served as a trustee for the boarding school at Stockbridge from 1743 to 1747, and the Northampton congregation, under Edwards' direction, heavily supported the work in the mid-1740s.[76]

As we shall see, not only did Edwards perform well in his pastoral duties to his congregations of English and Mohicans, but he also fought for the Indians' rights, attempting to ensure the government honored agreements made with them. This was at a time when settlers were eagerly searching for ways to swindle the Indians out of prime lands and holdings.[77] Lion Miles has done an excellent work chronicling how the settlers, and in particular the Williams family, schemed and crafted

---

[75] Marsden, *Jonathan Edwards*, 380–381.

[76] Nichols, "Last of the Mohican Missionaries," 49.

[77] My wife's grandfather, 9 generations back, named Teunis Cornelise Van Slingerlandt, came as a fur trader from Rotterdam, Netherlands in 1651. He settled in the Albany, NY area and in 1685 purchased 10,000 acres of property from the Indians for, "1 pieces of strands, 3 casks of rum, 3 kettles, 3 shirts, 159 hands white wampum, and 1 bag of powder." Part of that original property is still in family hands and today the town of Slingerlands is a suburb of Albany.

deals to their advantage, systematically forcing the natives out of the area and taking their land. One example will suffice:

> Two years later, in 1742, several Indians began to clear and fence a 70-acre tract with [John] Sergeant's encouragement. Ephraim Williams claimed this land for himself and ordered that the work be stopped. When the tribe protested, the General Court permitted Williams to keep the land, provided he pay the Indians £10 for their Labor.[78]

Such unethical practices had gone on long before Edwards arrival in 1751 and Miles refers to the time period from 1759 to 1774 as the "great land grab."

Having been systematically forced off their properties, in 1785 the remaining Mohicans moved to New York and named their settlement "New Stockbridge." It is interesting to note that during Edwards' time with them, the deceitful robbing of the Indians appears to have subsided somewhat. Nichols states, "The silence of Miles regarding the intervening years of 1751 to 1758, which correspond to Edwards' tenure at Stockbridge, reveals the lack of such a land grab under Edwards' watch and further evidences Edwards' attitude toward and treatment of the Stockbridge Mohicans."[79] This suggests that Edwards was committed to the total welfare of his Indian charges. Records indicate that during Edwards' tenure in Stockbridge, there were only five sales of Indian lands, whereas the following ten-year period after Edwards departed from Stockbridge in 1758, there were eighty-seven land transactions involving Mohican properties. Further evidence of Edwards' dedication to his ministry was the fact that unlike his predecessor, Sergeant, who built his house away from the Indians, on Prospect Hill, Edwards

---

[78] Lion G. Miles, "The Red Man Dispossessed: The Williams Family and the Alienation of Indian Land in Stockbridge, Massachusetts, 1736-1818." *The New England Quarterly* 68 (1994): 50.

[79] Nichols, "Last of the Mohican Missionaries," 53.

built his home in the midst of his Indian congregants so he could interact daily with them.[80] His living in close proximity to his charges was very effective and his son Jonathan Jr. states that at age six he became so fluent in the Mohican tongue that it was all he spoke outside the house:

> The Indians being the nearest neighbours, I constantly associated with them; their boys were my daily school mates and play fellows. Out of my father's house, I seldom heard any language spoken, beside the Indian. By these means I acquired the knowledge of that language, and a great facility in speaking it. It became more familiar to me than my mother tongue. I knew the names of some things in Indian, I did not know in English; even all my thoughts ran in Indian. [81]

Further evidence that Edwards was wholeheartedly committed to the wellbeing of the Mohicans is the fact that he purchased several small pieces of property in and around Stockbridge. The following are the deeds on file regarding his purchases: October 4, 1751-3 acres; December 5, 1751-8 acres; February 15, 1752-no acreage recorded; May 1, 1752-12 acres; February 19, 1754-5 acres and February 28, 1757-3 acres. The transcription of one of the key deeds to property Edwards' purchased will serve to prove a couple of key points.

> Edwards, Jonathan & Etowwohkaum. Jonas & Chanequin, James
> To All People to whom these presents shall Greeting Know Ye that we Jonas Etowwohkaum and James Chanequin both of Stockbridge in the County of Hampshire and Province of Massachusetts in New England Hunters and Indian

---

[80] In 1929 Sergeant's house was moved to its present location on the main street of Stockbridge. Edwards' home no longer exists, but a sundial marks its location.

[81] Jonathan Edwards, Jr., *Observations on the Language of the Muhhekaneew Indians* (New Haven: Josiah Meigs, 1788), preface.

Proprietors in the said Town of Stockbridge for and in consideration of the full and just sum of One Hundred Pounds Current Lawful Money of the Province of New York to us in hand well and truly paid before the Ensealing hereof by the said Rev. Mr. Jonathan Edwards his Heirs and Assigns "One certain Tract or Parcel of Land lying and being situate in & at said Stockbridge and lying on the street that leads thro the Plain to the Meeting House together with One Dwelling House and Barn standing on said Lot and is butted and bounded as follows, viz: Northwardly partly on land belonging to the Heirs of the Rev John Sergeant, and partly on Land of Mr. Josiah Jones, Westwardly on Thomas Sherman's land, Southwardly on the above said Street or Highway, Eastwardly on Land of Mohkkowuausut it being by estimation Eight Acres be it more or less. TO HAVE, and to hold the said granted and bargained Premises with all the Privileges and appurtenances thereto belonging or anywise appertaining to him the said Jonathan Edwards his Heirs and Assigns forever for ourselves, and Heirs quitting all claim. Right Title Challenge Interest Demand in or unto the said grants Land & Buildings forever free and clear of all other gifts, grants, bargains, sales, leans, Mortgages or conveyances of any kind Name or Nature whatsoever that in any way or manner obstruct or make void this Deed, as Witness our Hands, and seals this Fifth Day of December Anno Dom. One Thousand Seven Hundred, and Fifty One and in the Twenty Fifth Year of his Majesty's Reign George the Second King

Signed Sealed Delivered in presence of Timothy Woodbridge, Elias Willard, Jonas Etowwohkaum & seal, James Chanequin & seal Hampshire SS Stockbridge. We the subscribers pursuant to the Trust reposed in us by the vote of the General Court Oct:5th:1757 having informed and satisfied ourselves of the justice and equitableness of the sale, and purchase of the Land and buildings within mentioned do hereby signify our approbation thereof as Witness our Hands this 5th Dec. 1757. Joseph Pynchon, John Ashley Hampshire: SS: Stockbridge Sept:11:1751 Jonas Etowwohkaum and James Chanequin both of Stockbridge aforesaid severally acknowledged the foregoing Instrument to be their Act and Deed Joseph Dwight Justice of Peace Oct:14:1763 Rec'd and Recorded from the Original-Mark Hopkins, Reg'r[82]

Edwards purchased the above deeded property, just after agreeing to come to Stockbridge, from the sons of Umpachenee. As previously mentioned, Umpachenee and Konkapot were two of the early Mohican tribal leaders. The location of the property was key because it lay on the main street and was situated among the Indian settlers. But there were other reasons Edwards would procure property in the area. Since the property which he had originally been given access to in Northampton had been taken from the family, this meant he had nowhere to grow crops or graze animals. By purchasing property of his own, not only was he ensuring the welfare of his family, but he was also safeguarding against his future retirement, so that if need be, he could sell some. It should be noted that these were all small plots compared to the hundreds of acres that the settlers were obtaining.

Despite the setbacks in Stockbridge, the mission still held great potential for success. Part of this was due to the presence of the school. Marsden tells us, "The prospects were exciting because the new boarding school, under Captain Kellogg, had attracted the attention of tribes beyond the Mahicans."[83] With the threat of the French-English war looming, the British were eager to garner support from the Six Nations tribes in New York, especially their closest neighbors, the Mohawks. This enterprise also required Edwards' intervention, since it was being seriously mismanaged. Nichols states,

> Edwards handling of the "Indian School" at Stockbridge further reveals a distinction from his peers. Isaac Hollis, a "Baptist minister of means," was the chief patron of the school

---

[82] Berkshire Middle Registry of Deeds, Pittsfield, MA, Book 2, 239–241.
[83] Marsden, *Jonathan Edwards*, 382.

designated primarily to instruct Mohawks in both the English language and the Gospel.[84]

Given Ephraim Williams' character and history, it is not surprising that he was involved with Martin Kellogg in managing the running of the school. Edwards accused the two men of embezzling the school's funds — charge was ultimately proven to be true — and wrote many letters to those of influence among the commissioners in Boston, including Thomas Hubbard, Isaac Hollis, William Pepperell, and Joseph Paice. In the correspondence he outlined details of the mismanagement and pleaded with them to make changes before the Indians decided to resettle away from Stockbridge. Excerpts from one letter to Thomas Hubbard, dated March 30, 1752, will illustrate the issues and the passion with which Edwards attempted to effect change. He begins by recounting the circumstances upon which the school was begun under the first minister, John Sergeant and the procuring of Captain Martin Kellogg as schoolmaster. From here we go to Edwards' letter.

> Captain Kellogg, being a man in years above sixty-two and being lame and not well able to follow other business, was the more easily obtained; and so twelve boys were carried down here from Newington to be taken care of by Captain Kellogg at Mr. Hollis' charge [expense], where they continued a year. In the spring of the year 1749, the business being concluded, Captain Kellogg brought his boys hither.
> When Mr. Sergeant came to reckon with Captain Kellogg as agent for Mr. Hollis, he was extremely uneasy at some things in his conduct and accounts, and expressed a resolution to set things on some other foot, that more effectual care might be taken that Mr. Hollis should have justice done him in the expense of his money. But that summer, on July 27, Mr. Sergeant died before he had executed his design, and left the boys in Captain Kellogg's hands in the house intended for

---

[84] Nichols, "Last of the Mohican Missionaries," 55.

the boarding school, but in its first beginning and just sufficient to shelter them from the weather, where a kind of boarding school was kept, but in a very broken, confused manner, and nothing was taught the boys more than they might have been taught in a much better manner in the regular school that is maintained by the Commissioners under the care of Mr. [Timothy] Woodbridge, and no benefits received by them but what they would have had without any of that extraordinary [effort]. So that 'tis beyond dispute that Mr. Hollis' money was entirely thrown away.

The winter following began with great misunderstanding between Col. [Ephraim] Williams and Captain Kellogg on one side and Mr. Woodbridge on the other, which first began concerning Captain Kellogg and his manner of spending Mr. Hollis' money. The parents of Captain Kellogg's boys and the Indians of the town in general were extremely uneasy at Captain Kellogg's conduct and have often loudly complained in my hearing of Captain Kellogg's ill treatment of their children, and his neglecting them as to their board, clothing, and instruction, and why he little cares that their children should be kept clean and orderly. And by this means, the Indians of the town in general have been imbibed a deep prejudice against Captain Kellogg.

In that confused state things continued till the fall of the year 1750. And it then having been a considerable time since Captain Kellogg heard anything from Mr. Hollis, Captain Kellogg, supposing that he was dead, and that no further supplies were to be expected from him, dismissed all the boys. And some of the Mohawks being lately come, he applied himself wholly to the care of them, expecting his pay from the government. ...

Captain Kellogg at first seemed much animated by the Mohawks' coming and took a great deal of pains with them to teach 'em to read, but his method was unhappy. He set up no school but left the children to themselves, to come and read and go when they pleased. He never could be persuaded to go out of this way into a more regular method of teaching, though much pains has been taken with him to persuade him, and seemed by degrees to grow more and more negligent as the influence of the Mohawk affair diminished. ... The Mohawks have been very uneasy at this neglected and confused state of things relating to the instruction of their children and have grown more and more so, being desirous of a regular school and some proper method to bring their children to an amendment of manners. ...

Yea, I apprehend more than this. The Stockbridge Indians are in such a rustle and so uneasy by reason of some things belonging to the present state of affairs, that I think there is real danger that if there be no alteration, they, the great part of them, will break up and leave the town.[85]

Edwards lobbied vigorously to have the school put under his jurisdiction and even took some of the students into his own home to continue their schooling. After two years of fervent effort, his request was granted; by this time, however, the situation was irreparable. Nichols notes, "Before Edwards was named schoolmaster, however, the Mohawk chiefs resolved to leave Stockbridge. When the official word finally reached Stockbridge that Edwards was now in charge of the school, it had no pupils. Edwards reluctantly, but without any other choice, closed the school."[86] In a letter to the Reverend Thomas Prince, Edwards recounts:

When I received Mr. Hollis' letter, I proceeded with the greatest precaution and prudence I was capable of. I was here entrusted alone; but I took the best advice I could come at. When I informed Colonel Dwight of Mr. Hollis' orders, he offered to continue things along in the school in the state they were then in (if I would be at the charge of it) till I could be ready to take the care of them myself. ...

But as soon as I could, I sent for the Mohawks, all, men, women, and children to my house and desired the English people of the town that were my friends to be there, to be witnesses, and assisting in the conference. When all were met, I

---

[85] Claghorn, *The Works*, 16:460–470.
[86] Nichols, "Last of the Mohican Missionaries," 56.

told the Indians the orders I had from Mr. Hollis; made 'em the offer of taking their children; discoursed the matter very largely, some of my friends assisting me. I told 'em as much of the care I would take of their children as I thought was best. Mr. [Timothy] Woodbridge discoursed very largely to them, and used many arguments with them to induce 'em to leave their children under my care; told 'em what a probability there was that the school would be under better regulation than it had been. But they replied, that they had heard such promises concerning the school so often, and had been so often disappointed that they were discouraged; and moreover said the affair of their removal had been determined in a council of the sachems of their nation, which they could not depart from without carrying the affair to them again.[87]

While Edwards expended a considerable amount of his time and energy fighting for the physical well-being of the Indians, he spent an equal amount of time tending to their spiritual needs as well. While he was disturbed somewhat by the native rituals and paganism, he considered them to be less guilty than their English neighbors when it came to religious piety. His attitude toward the spiritual welfare of the Indians was quite different from many of his contemporaries, as McDermott tells us:

> The Jonathan Edwards who disdained native religion nevertheless held an extraordinarily positive view of the spiritual status of (some) Native American individuals and tribes, considered them to be less morally culpable than their white nominally Christian counterparts, and entertained and exalted conception of their eschatological destiny. Perhaps as a result of his seeing a spiritually receptive disposition in so many of them, he also held a more positive view of their humanity than most of his fellow colonials. Few of them desired anything but the extermination of the Indians, and certainly

---

[87] Edwards' letter to the Reverend Thomas Prince, May 10, 1754, Claghorn, *The Works*, 16:635-636.

not their salvation. ... Many of those contemporaries "distrusted and even opposed the missionary endeavor," judging Indians to be something less than fully human.[88]

In 1758 Edwards, after much deliberation and uncertainty, left Stockbridge to take the post of president of the College of New Jersey, now Princeton University. The presidency was left vacant when his son-in-law, Aaron Burr Sr. (1716–1757), husband of Esther Edwards, died on September 24, 1757. Jonathan's grandson, Aaron Burr, Jr., would become the third vice-president of the United States, under Thomas Jefferson. In 1804 while running for governor of the state of New York, Burr Jr. took offence at comments made by Alexander Hamilton and challenged him to a duel. Hamilton, one of the signatories of the Declaration of Independence, was mortally wounded and died on July 12, 1804. While Burr was never brought to trial, his political career came to an abrupt end after this event.

Edwards preached his first of two farewell sermons to the Mohicans on January 8, 1758. Shortly after his arrival in Princeton, a smallpox epidemic swept the area and Edwards, a believer in inoculation, received a vaccination. Edwards had often been ill and was never a very strong man and, after developing complications from the vaccine, succumbed on March 22, 1758, at age fifty-four. One of the last things he spoke was a message for his wife, Sarah, who had remained at Stockbridge with the younger children. To his daughters Esther and Lucy, at his bedside, he said:

> It seems to me to be the will of God that I must shortly leave you; therefore give my kindest love to my dear wife, and tell her, that the uncommon union, which has so long subsisted between us, has been of such a nature, as I trust is spiritual, and therefore will continue forever: and I hope she shall be

---

[88] Gerald R. McDermott, *Jonathan Edwards Confronts the Gods: Christian Theology, Enlightenment Religion, and Non-Christian Faiths* (Oxford: Oxford University Press, 2000), 201–202.

supported under so great a trial, and submit cheerfully to the will of God. And as to my children, you are now like to be left fatherless, which I hope will be an inducement to you all to seek a Father who will never fail you.[89]

Those gathered around his bed near the end began to speculate as to the future of the church and college once he had gone. Edwards' final words were, "Trust in God and ye need not fear."[90] After hearing of the death of her husband, Sarah penned a letter to their daughter Esther and said, "O what a legacy my husband, and your father, has left us."[91] Tragedy and heartache continued to afflict the family as only two weeks after Edwards died, his daughter Esther came down with a fever and died within a few days. Sarah, back in Stockbridge, herself became ill when she received the terrible news. By September she had regained sufficient strength to travel to Princeton to tend to her orphaned grandchildren, but as Marsden tells us, "Soon she contracted another illness and died on October 2, 1758."[92]

Edwards' Spirituality

All who have studied Edwards agree he was a multi-disciplined individual; he has been thought of as a great philosopher, teacher and theologian. McClymond and McDermott state,

> Jonathan Edwards was an activist, preacher, contemplative, missionary, philosopher, and theologian. He will be remembered for all these and more, but his most enduring legacy will be the theological vision that in profundity and influence has

---

[89] Haykin, *Jonathan Edwards*, 28.
[90] Samuel Hopkins, *Memoirs of the Life, Experience and Character of the Late Rev. Jonathan Edwards, A.M.* in *The Works of President Edwards* (1817 London ed.; repr. New York: Burt Franklin, 1968), I, 84.
[91] Iain H. Murray, *Jonathan Edwards-A New Biography* (Edinburgh: The Banner of Truth Trust, 1987), 442.
[92] Marsden, *A Short Life*, 132.

led many to regard him as the greatest religious thinker in the history of the Americas.[93]

As a precursor to analyzing some of the sermons he preached while in Stockbridge, his strength as a theologian will be demonstrated in a number of examples.

Resolutions
Scripture is what brought Edwards to faith, and his entire life and preaching would go on to be built on God's holy word. He stated that the Scriptures "are the light by which ministers must be enlightened, and the light they are to hold forth to their hearers; and they are the fire whence their hearts and the hearts of their hearers must be kindled."[94] Shortly after his spiritual awakening in the fall of 1722, Edwards wrote down 70 resolutions in an effort to keep himself diligent in the wake of his new-found faith. These resolutions were to serve as a reminder to Edwards to keep his thoughts on eternal things, to submit his will to God and do all for his glory. Marsden tells us, "His specific resolutions included trying to give up pride and vanity and trying to obtain strict discipline in eating and drinking, not to speak ill of others, and cultivating patience and serenity in place of anxiety."[95] Edwards was fully aware that in his own power he would be unable to fulfill these resolutions. In the preamble he clearly indicates, "Being sensible that I am unable to do anything without God's help, I do humbly entreat Him by His grace to enable me to keep the resolutions, so far as they are agreeable to His will, For Christ's sake."[96] In this statement Edwards

---

[93] McClymond and McDermott, *The Theology of Jonathan Edwards*, 23.

[94] Quoted in Michael A.G. Haykin, *A Sweet Flame: Piety in the Letters of Jonathan Edwards* (Grand Rapids: Reformation Heritage Books, 2007), 5.

[95] Marsden, *A Short Life*, 23.

[96] *The Resolutions of Jonathan Edwards*, 2006, https://www.desiringgod.org/articles/the-resolutions-of-jonathan-edwards (accessed February 13, 2018).

demonstrates his reliance on the Holy Spirit to enable him to uphold the resolutions.

It was his desire to read these resolutions over on a weekly basis and thereby keep them at the top of his mind. He well understood both the frailty and carnal nature in the heart of man; he also recognized that in order to stay within God's will and avoid the sins of "omission and commission," he must remain in God's Word. Marsden states, "High among his priorities were reminders not to omit his regular times of Scripture study and prayer and to control those passions that would distract his focus on God."[97] In his diary he recorded how he fared in his attempt to maintain his resolve. He did this not to indicate how well he was doing, but as a reminder of the working of God's Spirit in providing him with the grace to persevere.

What is interesting to note is that at the same time Benjamin Franklin (1706-1790) in Philadelphia, had also set up for himself a list of virtues toward the goal of living a good life. There was a stark difference between both the motivation and the outcome of the two men's documents, however. Marsden says, "Franklin's virtues were designed for self-fulfillment; Edwards's were designed to subordinate his own will to God's will."[98] What should also be noted is that while Edwards was consistently in God's Word daily, he does not make many explicit references to Scripture in the Resolutions, save for Resolution 32, (Proverbs 20:6); 62 (Ephesians 6:6-8); 64 (Romans 8:26 and Psalm 119:20), and 65 (Psalm 119). This by no means indicates that Scripture was not at the forefront of the writing of these resolutions, for a close examination of them reveals that they can only be accomplished through a strength of character produced by the Spirit (Galatians 5:22-23).

That Edwards was cognizant of his life purpose is clearly evident in Resolution 1, which says, "Resolved, that I will do whatsoever I think to be most to God's glory, and my own good, profit and pleasure,

---

[97] Marsden, *Jonathan Edwards*, 52.
[98] Marsden, *A Short Life*, 23.

in the whole of my duration, without any consideration of the time, whether now, or never so many myriads of ages hence."⁹⁹ In this bold statement he indicates that his life was to be lived for God's glory alone, and recognized that whatever happened was for his own good and according to the sovereign will of God. Edwards lived his whole life with a gospel focus, as was his stated desire in Resolution 18, "Resolved, to live so, at all times, as I think is best in my devout frames, and when I have clearest notions of things of the gospel, and another world."¹⁰⁰

An Humble Attempt
Edwards had witnessed two great periods of revival in New England: one in 1734–35, and one in 1740–42. He was convinced that these periods of revival were brought about by special seasons of prayer imploring God to send his Holy Spirit in renewed power upon the people. In an effort to capture his observations and thoughts on the subject, in 1748 he wrote *An Humble Attempt to Promote Explicit Agreement and Visible Union of God's People in Extraordinary Prayer, for the Revival of Religion and the Advancement of Christ's Kingdom on Earth, Pursuant to Scripture Promise and Prophecies Concerning the Last Time.* Haykin tells us, "This treatise had been inspired by information Edwards received during the course of 1745 about a prayer movement for revival that had been formed by a number of Scottish evangelical ministers."¹⁰¹ It was Edwards' desire that New England also be caught up in a new work of the Spirit and, while he attempted to implement a similar program in Northampton, it was to no avail. Marsden notes, "Edwards did everything he could to encourage the Concert among prayer societies in Northampton, but the town was in its spiritual doldrums and little came of it."¹⁰² In writing *An Humble Attempt*, Edwards sought to convince

---

⁹⁹ *The Resolutions of Jonathan Edwards* (accessed February 13, 2018).
¹⁰⁰ *The Resolutions of Jonathan Edwards* (accessed February 13, 2018).
¹⁰¹ Haykin, *Jonathan Edwards*, 31–32.
¹⁰² Marsden, *Jonathan Edwards*, 334.

the people, from Scripture, that by fervent prayer they could aid in ushering in the millennial kingdom of God, with its accompanying peace and joy.

The treatise is written in three parts. The first part is based on Zechariah 8:20–22, wherein Edwards gives a summary of the work of the Spirit through prayer. In the introduction he speaks of the glorious advancement of the church of God on earth and continues by reminding them that Scripture is clear that the future advancement will come from the fervent prayers of God's people. He then recounts the Scottish revival of 1744 and ends the section with the admonition, "If Persons who formerly agreed to this Concert, should now discontinue it; would it not look too like that Fainting in Prayer, against which we are so expressly warn'd in Scripture?"[103] In part two, Edwards begins by reminding his readers that the glory of the last days has not yet been realized. He says,

> It is evident from the Scripture, that there is yet remaining a great advancement of the interest of religion and the kingdom of Christ in this world, by an abundant outpouring of the Spirit of God, far greater and more extensive than ever yet has been.[104]

In part three, he describes the unspeakable joy and beauty that will be realized in the final kingdom and reminds them of the fact that part of the purpose of Christ's death was to provide the Holy Spirit: "The sum of the blessings Christ sought, by what he did and suffered in the work of redemption, was the Holy Spirit."[105] Edwards ends part three by

---

[103] Jonathan Edwards, *An Humble Attempt to promote explicit agreement and visible union of God's people in extraordinary prayer for the revival of religion and the advancement of Christ's Kingdom on earth, pursuant to Scripture-promises and prophecies concerning the last time* (Boston, New England: D. Henchman, 1747), 24.

[104] Edwards, *An Humble Attempt*, 26.

[105] Edwards, *An Humble Attempt*, 44.

providing many scriptural examples and motivations in an effort to convince his hearers as to why they should be involved in such an effort to pray. He concludes with,

> The encouragement to explicit agreement in prayer is great from such instances as these, but it is yet greater from those wonderful words of our blessed Redeemer, "I say unto you, that if any two of you shall agree on earth, touching any thing that they shall ask, it shall be done for them of my Father which is in heaven (Matthew 18:19)."[106]

Edwards raises possible objections to such a concert of prayer and systematically responds to each one using solid rational and scriptural grounds. To conclude the treatise, he cites the words of the great prophet,

> God will wipe away tears from off all faces, and the rebuke of his people shall he take away from off all the earth; for the Lord hath spoken it. And it shall be said in that day, Lo, this is our God, we have waited for him, and he will save us: this is JEHOVAH! we have waited for him, we will be glad and rejoice in his salvation. Amen (Isaiah 25:8, 9).[107]

Sinners in the Hands of an Angry God
Any discussion of Edwards' spirituality would be seriously lacking if it did not include a discussion and analysis of his most memorable sermon, "Sinners in the Hands of an Angry God." This is undoubtedly Edwards' most famous sermon; some would even say that it is the best sermon ever preached. Stout states, "'Sinners in the Hands of an Angry God' is arguably America's greatest sermon."[108] Marsden concurs

---

[106] Edwards, *An Humble Attempt*, 83.
[107] Edwards, *An Humble Attempt*, 188.
[108] Harry S. Stout, "Jonathan Edwards' Tri-World Vision," in *The Legacy of Jonathan Edwards,* D. G. Hart, Sean Michael Lucas, and, Stephen J, Nichols, eds. (Grand Rapids, Michigan: Baker, 2003), 44.

and on the very first page of his definitive work on Edwards says, "A heralded preacher, he delivered what became America's most famous sermon, *Sinners in the Hands of an Angry God.*"[109] As we have noted, Edwards was deeply affected by George Whitefield's preaching and the revivals that resulted not only in England but in America during his visit. Edwards knew that his oratorical skills were no comparison to those of Whitefield, whose strong booming voice had easily carried over Boston Common. Whitefield could also be very theatrical in his presentations and Roberts Liardon says, "George Whitefield—known as the 'Great Orator,' the 'Divine Dramatist,' and the 'Heavenly Comet' for his style and impact on all who heard him—was an evangelistic pioneer."[110] Liardon also states,

> From the beginning, Whitefield's preaching reflected years of theatrical performances and a heart filled with intense devotion. The pulpit was his stage, and he would use every ounce of intellect and talent to convey his sermon points. A famous actor of the time, David Garrick exclaimed, "I would give a hundred guineas if I could say, 'Oh' like Mr. Whitefield."[111]

Edwards, though not a dramatist, was gifted in rhetoric, and his knowledge and grasp of scriptural truths was unparalleled. His command of the English language, however, coupled with his strength in the classical languages meant he could paint word pictures that could stir the heart of his hearers. Subsequent to Whitefield's visit to America, it seems that Edwards altered his preaching style. Stout says, "By December 1740, unmistakable evidence appears in Edwards's manuscript sermons that he had begun to experiment and perfect his own revival rhetoric in Whitefield-like directions … Besides altering the

---

[109] Marsden, *Jonathan Edwards*, 1.

[110] Roberts Liardon, "George Whitefield," God's Generals, http://godsgenerals.com/georgewhitefiele/ (accessed February 18, 2018).

[111] Liardon, "George Whitefield" (accessed February 18, 2018).

form of his manuscript notes, Edwards shifted his content decisively from heaven to hell."[112]

Stout also mentions that in December of 1740 Edwards tried out his new sermon style and preached a sermon entitled, "Sinners in Zion," to his Northampton congregation. Stout continues, "Two weeks after preaching 'Sinners in Zion,' Edwards preached another 'Sinners' sermon: 'Sinners in the Hands of an Angry God.' It is not clear what effect this sermon had on his own congregation. Probably not much. After all, they had heard its substance only two weeks before."[113] It appears that another reason the sermon may not have had a dramatic effect was that Edwards did some revisions to it. "Edwards' original delivery of it to his Northampton congregation in June 1741 met with a muted reception. That was because the sermon, as first composed, was quite different, milder, and more pastoral." [114] Though this may have been the response of his Northampton congregation, Edwards would preach this sermon once more in Enfield, Connecticut on July 8, 1741, with very different results.[115]

However, though some would say this was Edwards' greatest sermon, others consider this sermon was one which severely damaged Edwards' image. Stephen Crocco stated,

> Nothing in Edwards' writings and reputation aided the decline, distanced him more from enlightened readers, and prevented him from having a wider hearing than his imprecatory sermons, particularly his widely published *Sinners in the Hands of an Angry God.*[116]

---

[112] Stout, "Edwards and Revival," 47.

[113] Stout, "Edwards and Revival," 48.

[114] Harry S. Stout and Nathan O. Hatch, eds., *The Works of Jonathan Edwards* (New Haven: Yale University Press, 2003), 22:400.

[115] Michael J. McClymond and Gerald R. McDermott, *The Theology of Jonathan Edwards* (Oxford: Oxford University Press, 2012), 427.

[116] Stephen D. Crocco, "Edwards's Intellectual Legacy," *The Cambridge Companion to Jonathan Edwards*, ed. Stephen J. Stein (Cambridge: Cambridge University Press, 2007), 303.

Let us now look at the sermon in some detail.

Edwards chose as his sermon text Deuteronomy 32:35, "Their foot shall slide in due time." He begins by reminding the audience that in this passage God is threatening to pour out his vengeance on his chosen people, the Israelites, who have been favored with his grace, and yet have not walked in his ways. He states that there are four inferences in this simple verse. First, "That they were always exposed to *destruction*; as one that stands or walks in slippery places is always exposed to fall."[117] One does not expect to fall, and yet when placed on slippery ground, the fall is unexpected and inevitable. The threat of imminent destruction for Israel has always been present and Edwards points to Psalm 73:18, "Surely thou didst set them in slippery places; thou castedst them down into destruction."

His second point is that one is always in danger of "sudden unexpected destruction." People walk about oblivious to the danger that is ever present and so, when their downfall comes, it is totally unexpected. He brings home this point by completing the thought from Psalm 73, quoting verse 19, "how they are brought into desolation as in a moment." The third point of his introduction is that people fall by themselves not by being pushed, but by the unexpected shifting of their own weight. He completes his introductory thoughts by stating that the only reason people have not yet fallen to destruction is that the right time for them has not yet come. Here Edwards draws on his knowledge of Greek and the difference between chronos (κρονος), which is the time of day, and chairos (καιρος), which means at just the proper moment. No doubt Edwards, thinking of God's perfect timing in all things, had in mind passages such as Romans 5:6 and Galatians 4:4, which state that at just the right time, God sent his son to redeem lost sinners. Edwards completes his introduction with the following declaration:

---

[117] *The Select Works of Jonathan Edwards* (London: Banner of Truth Trust, 1959), II, 183. Emphasis in original.

The observation from the words that I would now insist upon is this.—"There is nothing that keeps wicked men at any one moment out of hell, but the mere pleasure of God."—By the *mere* pleasure of God, I mean his *sovereign* pleasure, his arbitrary will, restrained by no obligation, hindered by no manner of difficulty, any more than if nothing else but God's mere will had in the least degree, or in any respect whatsoever, any hand in the preservation of wicked men one moment.[118]

At this point Edwards expounds on the foundation by presenting ten principles that can be taken from the passage in Deuteronomy. His first point is, "There is no want of *power* in God to cast wicked men into hell at any moment."[119] Edwards stresses that man neither has power within himself to stand against God, nor can anyone intervene for anyone else. He provides a vivid example of earthly man struggling to subdue someone who comes against him and notes that while it may take considerable strength to overcome an oppressor, this is not so with God. Of those who would stand against God he says, "They are as great heaps of light chaff before the whirlwind; or large quantities of dry stubble before devouring flames."[120]

Edwards' second point is that sinners "*deserve* to be cast into hell; so that divine justice never stands in the way."[121] He recalls that man's wickedness, sin and rebellion deserve an infinite punishment from a holy God and reminds them that the sword of divine retribution is always hanging above them and that there is nothing to prevent it falling except "the hand of arbitrary mercy, and God's mere will, that holds it back."[122] His third point reminds his audience that the sentence of condemnation has already been passed for those who have not embraced the grace of God and accepted Christ's atoning sacrifice. For evidence

---

[118] *The Select Works*, 184. Emphasis in original.
[119] *The Sermons*, Kimnach, Minkema & Sweeney, eds., 50. Emphasis in original.
[120] *The Select Works*, 184.
[121] *The Select Works*, 185. Emphasis in original.
[122] *The Select Works*, 185.

of this he goes to John 3:18, "He that believeth not is condemned already." In his fourth principle, Edwards says that those who are unsaved, "are now the objects of that very same *anger* and wrath of God, that is expressed in the torments of hell."[123] He tells them again that they are only still alive because of God's will and that his fierce anger is burning against them and is of such magnitude that it is greater than that which he feels toward those already in hell. It is here that he begins to aim his teaching directly at those seated before him:

> Yea, God is a great deal more angry with great numbers that are now on earth; yea, doubtless with many that are now in this congregation, who it may be are at ease, than he is with many of those who are now in the flames of hell... The wrath of God burns against them, their damnation does not slumber; the pit is prepared, the fire is made ready, the furnace is now hot, ready to receive them; the flames do now rage and glow. The glittering sword is whet, and held over them, and the pit hath opened its mouth under them.[124]

Edwards fifth point takes his audience into the realm where the principalities, powers, and rulers of the darkness dwell (Ephesians 6:12). He says, "The *devil* stands ready to fall upon them, and seize them as his own, at what moment God shall permit him."[125] He tells them that because of their wicked, sinful natures, their souls are already in the devil's possession and only God's restraint is now preventing their imminent departure into Satan's realm forever. The demons are also standing by, waiting in eager anticipation for the moment that God pronounces final judgment and that "if God should withdraw his hand, by which they are restrained, they would in one moment fly upon their poor souls."[126]

---

[123] *The Select Works*, 184. Emphasis in original.
[124] *The Select Works*, 185.
[125] *The Select Works*, 186. Emphasis in original.
[126] *The Select Works*, 186.

In his sixth point Edwards returns to the nature of man and the sin of Adam which inhabits all men from birth. "There are in the souls of wicked men those hellish principles reigning, that would presently kindle and flame out into hell-fire, if it were not for God's restraints. There is laid in the very nature of carnal men, a foundation for the torments of hell."[127] His lesson here is that the current wickedness of man is sufficient in and of itself both to start and to fuel the fires of hell and that God alone is the sole reason they have not yet been damned. He draws on Isaiah 57:20 which likens the human soul to a troubled sea, then goes to Job 32:11, "Hitherto shalt thou come, but no further: and here shall thy proud waves be stayed?" Once more he stresses to them that it is the saving grace of Almighty God which is keeping them from immediate destruction.

For his seventh point Edwards emphasizes that one cannot assume that because all is right and good for the present moment that it cannot be turned to disaster and eternal doom in the blink of an eye. Edwards notes,

> The unseen, unthought of ways and means of persons going suddenly out of the world are innumerable and inconceivable. Unconverted men walk over the pit of hell on a rotten covering, and there are innumerable places in this covering so weak that they will not bear their weight, and these places are not seen.[128]

Edwards' eighth principle is a simple one: no matter how careful we are, or how intelligent we are, we can neither save ourselves nor anyone else. He says that if intelligence were to play a role in preservation then there should be some obvious difference in the death rates of the wise, but such is not the case. Once more turning to Scripture he cites Ecclesiastes 2:16, "And how dieth the wise man? as the fool."

---

[127] *The Select Works*, 186.
[128] *The Select Works*, 187.

For his ninth point Edwards states, "All wicked men's pains and *contrivance* which they use to escape hell, while they continue to reject Christ, and so remain wicked men, do not secure them from hell one moment."[129] He explains that people go through life thinking that the good that they do will save them from judgment and eternal damnation. They continually try to convince themselves with the notion that the good they have done will be enough to preserve them from destruction. Edwards says these are deluded in thinking, and that hell is filled with those who were previously deluded by such thoughts.

His tenth and final point is that God is under no obligation to anyone and has made no promises except to those who have been saved by the blood of Christ. All of the rituals, prayers, and petitions made by carnal man will be for naught until they have accepted Christ as their savior.

Edwards summarizes this section of his sermon by reiterating each of the ten points and reminding them that for those yet unsaved, "the devil is waiting for them, hell is gaping for them, the flames gather and flash about them, and would fain hold on them, and swallow them up; the fire pent up in their own hearts is struggling to break out."[130]

The wording of the sermon up to this point is of a more general nature and Edwards has used nonspecific terms such as, "natural man" and "wicked men" to refer to the lost. As he moves into the application portion of his sermon, he gets more personal and directs his words at his present audience. At one point he hopes that "the use of this awful subject may be for awakening unconverted persons in this congregation. This that you have heard is the case of every one of you that are out of Christ."[131] He reminds them that the judgment of God is ever present on them and that at any moment they may be taken. Indeed, he stresses to them that they are a great and terrible burden to God's creation because of their sinful nature and that the weight of their sin pulls

---

[129] *The Select Works*, 187. Emphasis in original.
[130] *The Select Works*, 189.
[131] *The Select Works*, 189.

them toward their destruction. "Your wickedness makes you as it were heavy as lead, and to tend downwards with great weight and pressure towards hell."[132]

His metaphorical references to describing the constraint of God's wrath in this discourse are colorful and descriptive, and speaks of the sinner having no more power to keep himself from hell than a spider's web could stop a rock. He also mentions that God's wrath is like, "great waters that are dammed for the present."[133] At this point he reminds them that each and every day they are alive, their guilt increases in magnitude and the wrath of God accumulates in intensity. On reading this, one is immediately taken to the discourse between the ghost of Jacob Marley and Ebenezer Scrooge from Charles Dickens' *A Christmas Carol*. When asked why he is fettered with chains, Marley tells Scrooge that it is the burden he forged in life by neglecting others' needs and his ability to help. He then says to Scrooge, "Or would you know the weight and length of the strong chain you bear yourself? It was full as heavy and as long as this, seven Christmas Eves ago and you have labored on it since. It is a ponderous chain!"[134] So with each passing day apart from God's salvation, man accumulates more and more sin burden and his punishment increases. Edwards pleads with them to take stock of their current spiritual state before a God whose wrath is building on them and who is ready at any moment to open a floodgate of rage. He says,

> Thus all you that have never passed under a great change of heart, by the mighty power of the Spirit of God upon your souls; all you that were never born again, and made new creatures, and raised from being dead in sin, to a state of new, and

---

[132] *The Select Works*, 189.

[133] *The Select Works*, 189.

[134] Charles Dickens and Arthur Rackman (Illustrator), *A Christmas Carol* (New York: Weathervane Books [1977]), 27.

before altogether unexperienced, light and life, are in the hands of an angry God.[135]

At this moment Edwards reaches the crescendo of his sermon, describing, in the most graphic human terms he can muster, just how angry the Almighty and Holy God is with sinful, unregenerate people; more specifically, with those who have not bowed their knee and asked for mercy:

> The God that holds you over the pit of hell, much as one holds a spider, or some loathsome insect, over the fire, abhors you, and is dreadfully provoked: his wrath towards you burns like fire; he looks upon you as worthy of nothing else, but to be cast into the fire; he is of purer eyes than to bear to have you in his sight; you are ten thousand times more abominable in his eyes, than the most hateful venomous serpent is in ours.[136]

Edwards then brings the situation into a current time focus, reminding his hearers that it was only God's constraint that kept them from being taken while they lay down to sleep the night before, and it is only his mercy that is keeping them from being cast into hell while they sit in the pew before him. He pleads with them to consider their tenuous state at that very moment,

> O sinner! consider the fearful danger you are in: it is a great furnace of wrath, a wide and bottomless pit, full of the fire of wrath, that you are held over in the hand of that God, whose wrath is provoked and incensed as much against you, as against many of the damned in hell.[137]

He then focuses specifically on the wrath of God by expounding on four thoughts, again using Scripture to support his arguments. First,

---

[135] *The Select Works*, 191.
[136] *The Select Works*, 191.
[137] *The Select Works*, 191.

the wrath is that of an infinite God. Were it merely the wrath of an earthly monarch, it would be of little regard since the worst an earthly king could do would be to take their life. However, as God is infinite and holy, his wrath is of a much greater magnitude and will endure for eternity. For scriptural proof of this Edwards cites Luke 12:4, 5, "And I say unto you my friends, Be not afraid of them that kill the body, and after that have no more that they can do. But I will forewarn you whom ye shall fear: Fear him, which after he hath killed hath power to cast into hell; yea, I say unto you, Fear him." Next, he expounds on the magnitude and fierceness of God's wrath and presents five solid references to support his position. He starts by quoting Isaiah 59:18, which says, "According to their deeds, accordingly he will repay fury to his adversaries." Edwards then refers to Isaiah 66:15, "For behold, the Lord will come with fire, and with his chariots like a whirlwind, to render his anger with fury, and his rebuke with flames of fire." The point he is trying to stress is the intensity of the rage that God feels towards those who remain in their sinful state, in hopes of encouraging them toward salvation. Next, he calls on Revelation 19:15 which says that "he treadeth the winepress of the fierceness and wrath of Almighty God." Once more, before he adds more scriptural fuel to the fire, he pleads with those present to repent: "Consider this, you that are here present, that yet remain in an unregenerate state. That God will execute the fierceness of his anger, implies that he will inflict wrath without pity."[138] He reminds them that there is no reason why an infinite and holy God should feel any pity for them or grant them any mercy and must act out of justice and righteousness toward them.

Edwards then takes them to Ezekiel 8:18, "Therefore will I also deal in fury; mine eye shall not spare, neither will I have pity; and though they cry in mine ears with a loud voice, yet I will not hear them." He tells them that they can avoid such punishment by turning to God right at that very moment, and he will have mercy on them: "Now God stands ready to pity you; this is the day of mercy; you may

---

[138] *The Select Works*, 193.

cry now with some encouragement of obtaining mercy."[139] For those who will not call upon God for mercy, he reminds them that God says, as written in Isaiah 63:3, "I will tread them in mine anger, and will trample them in my fury, and their blood shall be sprinkled upon my garments, and I will stain my raiment."

Edwards' third point is simple: the wrath that God will inflict upon the wicked will be done to demonstrate to angels and men not only the magnitude of his love, but the fierceness of his wrath, that they might fall down in awe and worship of Almighty God. He tells them that if they continue in their present unconverted state,

> You shall be tormented in the presence of the holy angels, and in the presence of the Lamb; and when you shall be in this state of suffering, the glorious inhabitants of heaven shall go forth and look on the awful spectacle, that they may see what the wrath and fierceness of the Almighty is; and when they have seen it, they will fall down and adore that great power and majesty.[140]

He completes his description of God's wrath by stating that it will be everlasting. While it would be unimaginable for one to endure God's fury for the smallest moment, the unregenerate sinner will suffer it for all eternity. He asks them to consider a long future ahead that will stretch on for all eternity, filled with nothing but anguish and torment, and tells them, "There will be no end to this exquisite horrible misery."[141]

As Edwards concludes his thoughts, he reminds them of the urgency of their situation and how tenuous their current position is. As he stresses to them that they all know people who were just as sinful as they are that are now gone and are forever experiencing God's wrath, Edwards presses on them their hope of avoiding the same fate:

---

[139] *The Select Works*, 194.
[140] *The Select Works*, 195.
[141] *The Select Works*, 196.

> And now you have an extraordinary opportunity, a day wherein Christ has thrown the door of mercy wide open, and stands calling, and crying with a loud voice to poor sinners; a day wherein many are flocking to him, and pressing into the kingdom of God.[142]

He then paints a contrasting picture between the joy of those who have been saved with those who miss Christ's call. He adds to the sense of urgency by referring to the revival that has come to the Connecticut Valley, telling them that God has been bringing more people into his kingdom and compares it to the outpouring of the Holy Spirit during the apostolic age. In his final thoughts he becomes very personal, no doubt making eye contact with as many as he can, as he proclaims,

> Therefore, let every one that is out of Christ, now awake and fly from the wrath to come. The wrath of Almighty God is now undoubtedly hanging over a great part of this congregation. Let every one fly out of Sodom: "Haste and escape for your lives, look not behind you, escape to the mountain, lest you be consumed."[143]

As mentioned previously, Edwards had preached this sermon once before to his Northampton congregation with no apparent effect. This was not the case in Enfield as, partway through the sermon, people began to weep, wail and shriek as they thought of God's wrath upon them. Several times Edwards was interrupted in his presentation and the situation became so disrupted that he was unable to finish the sermon! Stephen Williams, a pastor from Longmeadow, about five miles from Enfield, was in attendance at the service and afterwards recorded the experience in his diary.

> Went over to Enfield, where we met Dear Mr. Edwards of New Haven who preached a most awakening Sermon from

---

[142] *The Select Works*, 197.
[143] *The Select Works*, 199.

those words Deut 32:35—and before ye Sermon was done there was a great moaning and crying out throughout ye whole house. What shall I do to be saved—oh I am going to Hell—oh what shall I do for a Christ etc. etc.—so that ye minister was obliged to desist. [The] shrieks and crys were piercing and Amazing. After some time of waiting the congregation were still so that a prayer was made by Mr. W—and after that we descended from the pulpit and discoursed with the people—some in one place and some in another. And Amazing and Astonishing [was] ye power. God was seen and severall souls were hopefully wrought upon that night and oh ye cheerfulness and pleasantness of their countenances ..."[144]

Why did this sermon have such a profound effect on the Enfield people, when weeks earlier it had apparently fallen on deaf ears in Northampton? Certainly, it was not due to any theatrics or Edwards' passionate delivery. His own contemporary, Thomas Prince, in 1744 stated that Edwards' style had a "... natural way of delivery, and without any agitation of body, or anything else in the manner to excite attention."[145] George Marsden agrees and tells us,

> Edwards was not like Whitefield, who could win over a congregation by free-wheeling dramatic eloquence. His voice was weak, and he preached from a full manuscript that he had virtually memorized ... In the case of "Sinners," unlike most of his sermons, he added extensive vivid imagery. The combination proved overwhelming.[146]

Even though Edwards softened his original Northampton manuscript before he preached it at Enfield, its impact on the Connecticut congregation was overwhelming. McClymond and McDermott state,

---

[144] Stout, "Edwards and Revival," 49.
[145] Quoted in Iain Murray, *Jonathan Edwards: A New Biography* (Carlisle, PA.: Banner of Truth, 1987), 175.
[146] Marsden, *A Short Life*, 66.

"It would seem that the original sermon's wording was tempered a bit when compared to the version we now have in print. Kimnach says the sermon given at Enfield, 'preserves a wise balance between the carrot and the stick,' unlike the versions most Americans have read."[147] Carse believes that Edwards' focus was not so much on hell as it was on the uncertain time with which death and judgment would fall and states:

> The most famous of all Edwards' sermons, "Sinners in the Hands of an Angry God," is not properly a description of hell as such. It is concerned rather with the fact that the time between the present and one's death is a totally unknown quantity. Death comes suddenly and unannounced ... The imagery of the sermon is designed to communicate the sense of a disaster close at hand.[148]

It seems that Edwards' gifted use of the English language and his superb ability to draw word pictures in allegory was used by the Holy Spirit to effect a dramatic conviction in the hearts of the congregation at Enfield. His metaphors included "The black clouds of God's wrath," "great waters that are dammed," "the bow of God's wrath is bent," "Your wickedness makes you heavy as lead," "Unconverted men walk over the pit of hell on a rotten covering," "God holds you over the pit of hell, much as one holds a spider." Edwards' preaching style may have been simple and undramatic but his rhetorical genius was nowhere better illustrated than here.[149]

---

[147] McClymond and McDermott, *The Theology of Jonathan Edwards*, 509.

[148] James Carse, *Jonathan Edwards & The Visibility of God* (New York: Charles Scribner's Sons, 1967), 156.

[149] Harry S. Stout ed., *The Works*, 22:401.

5
SELECTIONS FROM THE SERMONS OF JONATHAN EDWARDS TO THE STOCKBRIDGE MOHICAN INDIANS

Jonathan Edwards' first sermon to his Mohican congregation was given in a starkly different manner and venue than his predecessor, John Sergeant. Sergeant had first met the Mohicans in the woods where they were camped and preached his first message to them on October 13, 1734, through an interpreter. As previously noted, Sergeant's message touched the heart of his interpreter, Ebenezer Poohpoonuc, who became one of the first baptized converts of the mission. When Edwards arrived in Stockbridge in 1751, however, though he did so to an established congregation he was at a disadvantage, since he did not speak the Mohican language. Sergeant had taken great pains to learn the Mohican tongue and they would have been used to being preached to in their native language without the mediation of an interpreter. While Edwards' son, Jonathan Jr., became fluent in Mohican to the point of writing a book on it,[1] Edwards never did learn, and preached through an interpreter for his entire tenure with the tribe. It is difficult to evaluate how this handicap may have affected the efficacy of his sermons, for much can be lost in translation, including emphasis on words, the use of clichés, and appropriate inflection of voice to make a point. Also affecting delivery of his sermons would be the misinterpretation of his

---

[1] Jonathan Edwards, Jr., *Observations on the Language of the Muhhekaneew Indians* (New Haven: Josiah Meigs, 1788).

mannerisms by the Indians and the possibility that some may even have been offensive to them.

Though Edwards' interpreter, John Wauwaumpequuanaunt, would occasionally drink to excess, Edwards was generally pleased with his service as translator. Frazier comments,

> Edwards warmly praised him, describing him as "on some accounts, an extraordinary man, understands English well, is a good reader and writer, and an excellent interpreter." Edwards boasted that perhaps no other educated American Indian better understood divinity and the scriptures.[2]

Whatever disadvantages Edwards may have experienced due to his personal deficiency in being able to communicate directly, he made up for in his personal diligence to preach God's Word. Wheeler notes:

> During his tenure at Stockbridge, from his official installation in August 1751 until he was offered the post as president of Princeton in the fall of 1757, Jonathan Edwards ascended the pulpit hundreds of times to preach to the Stockbridge Indians.; he also wrote dozens of letters to government and mission society officials in the effort to defend Indian interests against abuse. Edwards does not seem to have developed any close relationships with the Stockbridge Indians, but this might be said of the whole of his life, not just his Stockbridge years. Yet Edwards was profoundly affected by his experience at the mission, contrary to the popular and scholarly image of the reclusive scholar too busy producing his masterworks to be overly concerned with the daily affairs of the mis-

---

[2] Patrick Frazier, *The Mohicans of Stockbridge* (Lincoln: University of Nebraska Press, 1992); Rachel Wheeler, *To Live Upon Hope* (Ithaca, New York: Cornell University Press, 2008), 94.

sion. Perhaps, unexpectedly, despite the nearly constant battles, his post at Stockbridge may well have been his most rewarding ministry.[3]

The fact that there has been a significant amount of material written on the life and ministry of Edwards in recent years suggests that his work continues to be important even today. Despite the volumes of material available on Edwards, however, very few of his sermons to the Mohicans have ever been published. The remainder of this work will hopefully fill some of that void.

The First Sermon-January 1751[4]
What is most likely Edwards' first sermon to the Mohicans was preached to them in January of 1751. He chose as his text Acts 11:12-13, and it is entitled "The Things That Belong To True Religion."

THE THINGS THAT BELONG TO TRUE RELIGION

Acts 11:12-13
And the spirit bade me go with them, nothing doubting. Moreover these six brethren accompanied me, and we entered into the man's house: and he showed us how he had seen an angel in his house, which stood and said unto him, Send men to Joppa, and call for Simon, whose surname is Peter.

---

[3] Rachel Wheeler, *To Live Upon Hope* (Ithaca, New York: Cornell University Press, 2008), 7.

[4] The sermons will be presented as transcribed and on file at the Beinecke Rare Book and Manuscript Library at Yale University. Spelling and grammar are unchanged and if words have been stroked out in the original, they have not been included. Some words and punctuation which were obvious and excluded in the original have been added, and the text reformatted for readability. This transcription is numbered 976 in the Jonathan Edwards Center at Yale. This sermon was published in Wilson H. Kimnach, ed., *The Works of Jonathan Edwards* (New Haven: Yale University Press, 2006) 25:566-575. Used with permission of Yale University Press.

We have an account in the Bible, in Acts 11:12-13, [of] how there was a man whose name was Cornelius, [who] was praying to God; and an angel appeared to him, and the angel bid him send to a town called Joppa for one of Christ's ministers, who was called Peter.

And the angel told him, this Peter shall tell him words by which he and all his family shall be saved.

Before Christ came into the world, there was but one nation in the world—the nation of the Jews—that had the true religion. All other nations were heathen for about 1500 years.

When Christ lived in the earth, he chose twelve men to go along with him wherever he went, that he might teach 'em and instruct 'em, and fit 'em to be ministers of the gospel. Peter was one of these twelve ministers. After Christ was crucified and rose from the dead, he bid his disciples go and preach the gospel to other nations besides the Jews: to go all over the world and to teach the true religion.

And the disciples did as Christ bid 'em. They went all over the world, and a great many turned to the true God and to the Christian religion all over the world.

Now Peter was the first of those twelve ministers that I told you Christ chose, that preached the gospel to other people besides the Jews. This Peter was the man that came and preached the gospel to Cornelius. This Cornelius was not a Jew; he was one of another nation, of a nation that used to be heathen. He belonged to a nation that had conquered the Jews. He was a captain that had soldiers under him, and was sent into the Jews' country to keep 'em in subjection.

He had heard something of the true God before Peter came to him, but he knew but little; he did not know anything about Jesus Christ. But he was willing to be instructed: he had a mind to know more, and therefore he prayed to God that he might be brought into the light; and while he was at prayer, God heard his prayer and sent an angel to tell him how he should come into greater light.

He bid him [send] men to a town called Joppa, where Peter was who should instruct him and his family so that they might all be saved. And he did so, and Peter came to him and instructed him concerning

Jesus Christ, and they all gladly received the word and it filled 'em full of joy to hear concerning Jesus Christ, the Savior of men.

And when they heard Peter preach about Christ, they gave up their hearts to Jesus Christ and became good Christians. And Cornelius and his family was the first of other nations besides the Jews that Christ's ministers preached the gospel to. And after that they preached the gospel to others in all parts of the world, so that after a while a great many nations turned Christian. And after this the English nation had the gospel preached to 'em and turned Christian, who before were heathen.

Now I am come to preach the true religion to you and to your children, as Peter did to Cornelius and his family, that you and all your children may be saved. And I hope that you will mind what I say to you, and joyfully receive my words as Cornelius did the words of Peter.

Now, therefore, I'll tell you what true religion is, and what that religion is that you must have if ever you are saved. True religion don't consist in praying to the Virgin Mary and to saints and angels. It don't consist in crossing themselves, in confessing sins to the priest, and worshipping images of Christ and of the saints, and other things that the French do. Nor does true religion consist chiefly in being baptized, going to church and coming to sacraments: good Christians should do these things, but these ben't the chief things in true religion.

[DOCTRINE.]
But these things which I am now going to tell you of belong to true religion.

One thing is to be instructed [to] understand what the true God is, to know and understand Christ and the way how God saves men by Christ, and to know about another world.

Another thing is to have the eye opened to see the excellency of those things which the Bible teaches about God and Jesus Christ, to taste the sweetness of 'em, and have those things sink down into the heart.

Another thing is to believe the things which the Bible teaches about God and Christ and another world to be certainly true: to have 'em seem not like a dream or an idle story, but like real things. In order to men's being truly religious, they must see how they have sinned against God and made God angry: [they must see] what wicked creatures they [are], must see what wicked hearts they have, and [that they] are all over wicked. [They must see that they] deserve that God should hate 'em and should take 'em and cast 'em into hell and show 'em no mercy.

In order to be good Christians, men must see what poor, miserable creatures they be, and can't help themselves, and [that] they need Christ to pity and help 'em and be their Savior.

[They] must see that they can never do anything to make satisfaction for their sins, or pay God for their sins they have committed against him, and that they need Christ to make satisfaction for 'em by his precious blood.

[They must have] new hearts given to 'em.

And then they must have their eyes opened to see how lovely Christ is and that he is just such a Savior as such poor creatures as they want. And their hearts must go to Christ. They must come to Christ with all their hearts to save 'em. They must give their hearts to Christ, and with all their hearts give themselves to him, to be some of his people forever and ever.

They must love God and Christ better than father or mother, wife and children, brothers or sisters; yea, better than all the world. They must love the word of God and love the ways of God: love all goodness.

'Tis to hate all sin, all drunkenness, lying and cheating, revenge and malice, and all ways of wickedness.

'Tis to repent of their sins, to be sorry and grieved, and mourn for sin and have the heart broken for sin.

'Tis to turn from drunkenness and lying and all wicked ways, and [to] live a holy life, keeping all the commandments of God as long as they live.

'Tis to pray to God: they must go alone and pray to him every day, and to pray to him with the heart.

Keep the sabbath: not to hunt nor to work nor to play a sabbath, but spend the time in praying, going to meeting, and thinking and talking about the things of religion.

And all these things must be done with the heart.

Love good people that are the people of Christ: to love 'em as brothers and sisters, to have the heart joined to all such. Love all men: endeavor to do good to all, and not to do any hurt to any.

'Tis not to be proud, but to be a humble spirit, like Jesus Christ, who though he was the great God yet became a man and was a friend of poor men, and eat and drank with them, and instructed 'em and never despised any.

To be of a peaceable, quiet, mild spirit: not to be apt to be angry and quarrelsome, but to love to live peaceably with all.

Not to revenge upon those that offend us, do us hurt, but to do good for evil; because Christ loved us and did us good and died for us, though we have done much evil to him and sinned against him.

They that have true religion have their hearts taken off from the things of this world and have their hearts in heaven.

[They] are like a child that is weaned from the mother's breast, so they are weaned from all the good things of this world; they don't set their hearts on those things.

Heaven is their country, 'tis their Father's house: there they choose their portion and inheritance. They are a-going a journey to heaven, and though they may have a great deal of trouble and labor by the way, and may be very weary, yet heaven is their resting place.

And in all these things we must give God our hearts: God sees the heart and he looks at the heart. It will signify nothing to do a great many things outwardly, if we don't give God our hearts.

[APPLICATION.]

These things that I have told you are the true Christian religion. Such things as these will make men good men.

If men han't such religion as this, it will never do being baptized, and coming[5] to sacraments will never save 'em.

Such as [practice] this religion will surely go to heaven when they die.

They that han't such religion will go to hell, if they are baptized or unbaptized, come to sacraments or no.

This is the religion that Jesus Christ came into the world to teach men.

Those only are true Christians. Jesus Christ won't own any other but such as these to be his people in another world; all others he'll set along with the heathen.

This is the religion that the Bible teaches, and you should try that your children may learn English that they may read the Bible and there learn this religion.

This is the religion that I will teach you while I stay in this place. This religion will make men good one to another, teach 'em to do good and to do no hurt, [make them] comfortable and pleasant to all men while in this world.

Such as have this religion are happy men; they need not be afraid to die: death can do 'em no harm.

God loves such men and is their Father, and will take care of 'em; and Christ loves 'em and their souls are married unto Jesus Christ, and Christ is the husband of their souls.

There is none can do such any harm if they hate 'em: if they kill 'em, yet they can't do 'em any hurt, for when they die they go to a better country.

The devil will try all that he can to keep you from such religion as this.

When men, as they are born, first come into the world, they have no such religion as this in their hearts, but their hearts are full of all manner of wickedness. They that have true religion, therefore, are all born again. God gives 'em new hearts and makes 'em new men.

---

[5] Original manuscript says "come."

Therefore, you must every day, all of you, go alone and pray to the great God that he will enlighten your minds and give you new hearts, that you may have true religion.

And you that are fathers and mothers, you should often talk to your children and give 'em good counsel, that they mayn't go in the ways of sin and wickedness; but they may pray to God to give 'em new hearts and make 'em truly religious.

In this sermon, Edwards' approach was to begin with a narrative, follow it with several points of doctrine, and finally summarize how they should apply the biblical principles to their own lives. Though at this point the Mohicans had been living under the capable ministry of John Sergeant for fifteen years, Edwards begins with a basic introduction to the history of Christianity. He begins with introducing Cornelius, a spiritual man, who prayed to God. Edwards explains, "This Cornelius was not a Jew; he was one of another nation, of a nation that used to be heathen." Here he is setting up a similarity between the Mohicans and Cornelius. He goes on to say of Cornelius, that "He had heard something of the true God before Peter came to him, but he knew but little; he did not know anything about Jesus Christ."

Next, Edwards' gives a brief synopsis of the history of true religion in the world, telling them that one nation alone, the Jews, had the truth about God and that all others were heathens. He tells them that Christ came into the world to teach about this true religion and also began with the Jews. Edwards follows with an introduction to Peter, describing him as one of the twelve who were chosen by Christ to spread the Good News. However, Peter's ministry differed from Christ's in that he was the first disciple to take the gospel to those who were not of his own race. The similarity of Peter to the missionaries who came to the Indians can be readily deduced from the description given. Edwards acknowledges that the spread of the gospel began with Cornelius and his family, and spread to all nations resulting in the English being converted: "And after this the English nation had the gospel preached to 'em and turned Christian, who before were heathen." He then points to himself as a saved Englishman, entrusted with the same mission to the Indians that Peter had to Cornelius, "Now I am come to preach the true religion to you and to your children, as Peter did to Cornelius and his family, that you and all your children may be saved."

Edwards also takes the opportunity to warn the Mohicans against the doctrines of the Roman church, which they would have been exposed to through contact with other Canadian tribes that had come under the teaching of the French Jesuits. He tells them that true religion is not found in outward expressions such as making the sign of the cross, nor in worshiping idols "and other things that the French do." He finishes his narrative by reminding them that true religion and salvation will not be found in the rituals of baptism and communion, and notes that while it is important for devoted, professing Christians to partake of the sacraments, these do not lead to salvation. By making this point abundantly clear at the outset of his ministry, he was no doubt trying to avoid the major issue that had been his bane in Northampton.

From the narrative, Edwards moves to the doctrinal meaning of the passage and proceeds to explain to them what he means by true religion. He tells them that merely hearing the words of Scripture is not enough. Rather, they need to let the words "sink down into the heart," and thereby know at a heart level that Jesus Christ is truth. Here Edwards falls back on his favorite description of God and his Word, when he instructs them "to taste the sweetness of 'em." He goes on to say that the truth of Scripture must cause them to look at themselves and see how utterly sinful they are when compared to the holiness of God, and to acknowledge that there is no good in them. He states that "they must see how they have sinned against God and made God angry: [they must see] what wicked creatures they [are], must see what wicked hearts they have, and [that they] are all over wicked." After informing them that there is nothing they can do about their naturally wicked state, he moves on to the good news that God sent Jesus to be their Saviour. He stresses the fact that they must give *all* to Christ; this includes giving up their previous sinful practices, and specifically mentions drunkenness twice—the sin that had most plagued the Mohicans.

From here Edwards lists some attributes and actions of the one who has given his heart fully to God. These include the importance of being people of daily prayer, as well as being those who attend the Sabbath meetings and who also refrain from idle activities, including hunting, during that day. They are also to be those who demonstrate love to all, especially to those in God's family, and to strive to live peaceably with everyone. He focuses especially on the importance of not seeking revenge when they have been wronged and presumably may have been aware of several instances of retributive acts towards other Indians in the past. He reminds them that even though they have wronged Jesus most severely, yet he loved them to the point of giving his life for them; for this reason, he says, they should act in a similar manner towards those who would treat them badly, and return evil with good. He closes off the doctrinal portion of his sermon with a reminder that to be a Christian does not mean their lives will be free of trouble, but that despite whatever trouble may come, their final home is in heaven.

In his final section, Edwards attempts to give some practical applications. He explains that the true religion he is preaching to them can only be realized as they give their whole heart to God and live according to his commands. Attending services and going through the rituals of baptism and communion are ultimately insufficient to get them to heaven: "They that han't such religion will go to hell, if they are baptized or unbaptized, come to sacraments or no." Another interesting application is Edwards' encouragement to the Mohicans to ensure their children learn English so they can read the Bible and learn firsthand of Christianity: "This is the religion that the Bible teaches, and you should try that your children may learn English that they may read the Bible and there learn this religion."

What is noteworthy is that Edwards does not go into a detailed description of hell as a place of eternal, intense torment, as he had with his sermon, "Sinners in the Hands of an Angry God." It may be that, as this was his first discourse to the Mohicans, he was endeavouring to keep his message plain, simple and direct. He closes with the encouragement that, should they practice the religion he will teach them, they will live good, happy lives, and need not ever fear death.

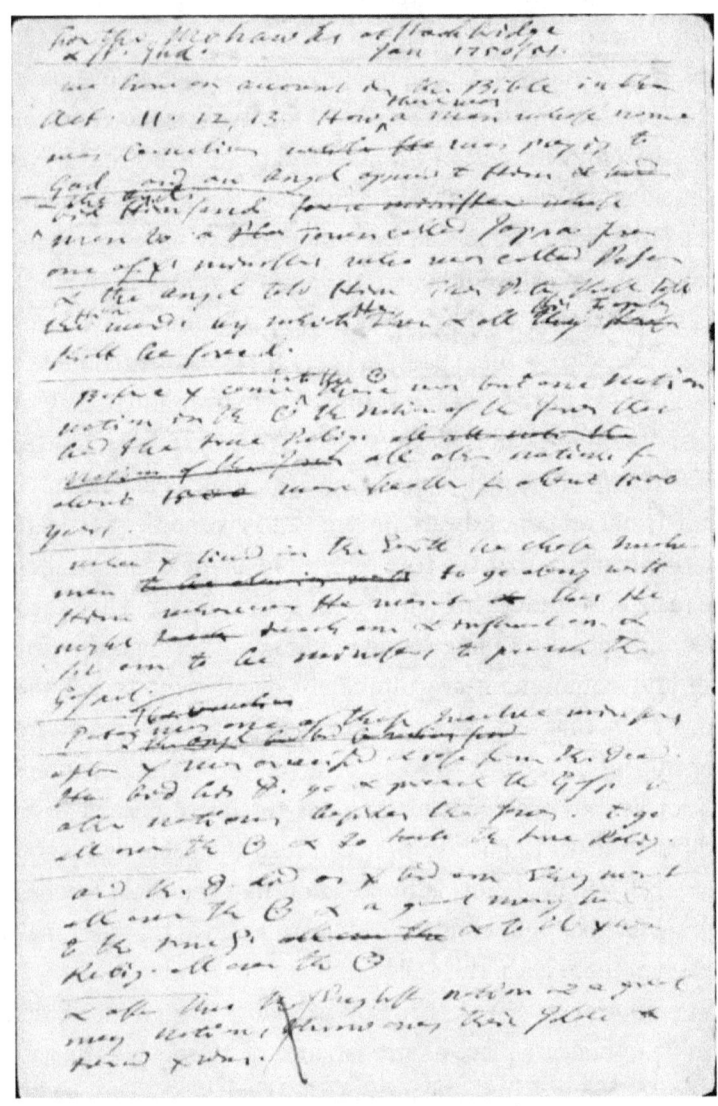

First page of Edwards' "The Things That Belong To True Religion" preached January 1751. Beinecke Rare Book and Manuscript Library-Yale University

Sermons

Sermon to the Mohicans & Mohawks at the Treaty, August 16, 1751
In August of 1751 a delegation of government officials and representatives of the Mohawk Indians came to Stockbridge in an effort to secure a treaty with the Mohawks, and to convince some of them to move to Stockbridge and have their children attend the school. This was a strategic political alliance on the part of the English, for there was impending war with the French in Canada and it was essential to solidify a Mohawk allegiance. The French had already been successful in wooing the Iroquois nation to their side as the Catholic Jesuits had been actively proselytizing among them. Seizing upon this dual political and spiritual platform, Edwards preached to the group on Friday, August 16, 1751.[6]

TO THE MOHAWKS AT THE TREATY
August 16, 1751

II Peter 1:19
We have also a more sure word of prophecy, whereunto ye do well that ye take heed, as unto a light that shineth in a dark place, until the day dawn, and the day star arise in your hearts.

When God first made man, he had a principle of holiness in his heart.

That holiness that was in him was like a light that shone in his heart, so that his mind was full of light.

But when man sinned against God, he lost his holiness, and then the light that was in his mind was put out.

Sin and the devil came in and took possession of his heart, and his mind was full of darkness.

---

[6] This sermon is published in *The Sermons of Jonathan Edwards, A Reader*. Wilson H. Kimnach, Kenneth P. Minkema & Douglas A. Sweeney, eds. (New Haven: Yale University Press, 1999), 105-110. This transcription is numbered 1002 at the Jonathan Edwards Center at Yale. Used with permission of Yale University Press.

But the consequence was that the world of mankind sank down more and more into darkness, and most of the nations of the world by degrees quite lost the knowledge of the true God.

Some worshipped [the] sun and moon and stars, some worshipped images of gold and silver, brass and iron, wood and stone.

Some worshipped serpents and other beasts.

And some worshipped the devil, that used to come to 'em, and appear to 'em, and make 'em believe he was the one true God.

And other nations that had some remembrance of the God that made the world yet were very much in the dark. They did not know what he was.

Knew very little about another world and what was like to become of men after they are dead.

Nor did they know anything, how men that had sinned and had offended God should be reconciled to him and obtain his favour.

And many more nations were very ignorant and blind and did not know much more than the beasts.

In this state the world was very miserable, not knowing anything, what they should do to be saved.

And so the greater part of the world from generation to generation was blinded by the devil and led down to destruction.

But the great God took pity on mankind and gave 'em the holy Scriptures to teach men and to be in this world as a light shining in a dark place.

God first made known himself to Moses and other prophets, and directed them to write a part of the Bible.

And after many ages, he sent his own Son into the world to die for sinners and more fully to instruct the world.

This was about 1,750 years ago.

And then Christ directed his apostles to write the Word in a more clear manner, and so the Bible was finished.

And Christ commanded that his word contained in the Bible should be oped to all nations, and that all should be instructed out of it.

And this is the great light that God has given to teach mankind concerning the God that made 'em and concerning another world.

Now those nations that have the Scripture, they enjoy light. The Lord Jesus shines upon them like a bright and glorious sun.

But the nations that have not the Bible live in great darkness, and the devil, the prince of darkness reigns over 'em.

But here you must note this: of them that have the Bible, there are two sorts.

There are some that are truly good men, and they not only have the light shining round about 'em, but the light shines into their hearts.

And there are others that are wicked men that will not regard the Scripture, and they, although the light shines round about 'em, yet it don't shine into 'em but are perfectly dark within.

Those last receive no benefit by the Scripture. The Scripture does 'em no good.

But 'tis their own fault. They have great opportunity to be made happy if they would but improve it.

Therefore there are these two things one ought to do:

1. We should seek to know the Word of God, that we might be instructed by it.

2. We should receive it into our hearts and practice according to it.

Now, therefore mind the Apostle's counsel in the text. Give heed to this sure word of God till "the day dawn, and the day start arise in your hearts."

Your forefathers have for a great many ages lived in great darkness.

And since the whiter people came over the seas and have settled in these parts of the world, they have not done their duty to you. They have greatly neglected you.

So that although 'tis about 140 years since the white people came over here, there are but a few of the poor Indians have been thoroughly instructed to this very day.

But few of your children have been taught to read.

And therefore you know but little of the Word of God, for you ben't able to read it.

This has been a shameful neglect of the white people, by which the great God has undoubtedly been made very angry.

For God is a merciful God, and would have all men be saved and come to the knowledge of the truth.

Jesus Christ gave command that the gospel should be preached to all nations.

The Christian religion teaches kindness and love to all mankind.

And therefore the white people have not behaved like Christians, that they have shown no more love to your souls.

The French, they pretend to teach the Indians religion, but they won't teach 'em to read. They won't let 'em read the Word of God. They are afraid if they should read the Scripture, they would know that their ways are not agreeable to the Scripture.

And therefore they refuse to open the Bible to the Indians, but keep it just shut up.

When the Bible is hid from 'em, they can cheat 'em and make 'em believe what they have a mind to.

And many of the English and Dutch are against your being instructed. They choose to keep you in the dark for the sake of making a gain of you.

For as long as they keep you in ignorance, 'tis more easy to cheat you in trading with you.

And some have taken wrong ways in instructing the Indians.

And they have baptized 'em and given the sacrament to 'em before they have been well instructed, and while they have lived in their drunkenness.

Whereas baptism and the sacrament are privileges which God has appointed only for his people, such as are virtuous men.

And no wonder many white people flatter the Indians in their wickedness: for they live in wickedness and flatter one another in it.

But you have been neglected long enough. 'Tis now high time that some more effectual care should be taken that you may be really brought into the clear light, and know as much as the English do.

And the great God seems mercifully to have moved the hearts of many of the English of late, especially in England, to give much money for this end.

And we do no more than our duty in it, for it was once with our forefathers as 'tis with you. They formerly were in great darkness and knew no more that the Indians when the white people forst came over here.

But God put it into the hearts of others to come and instruct the English in the Word of God, and so to bring 'em into the light.

This good we had by the kindness of God to us, and therefore we ought to be ready to show this kindness to you.

We are no better than you in no respect, only as God has made us to differ and has been pleased to give us more light. And now we are willing to give it to you.

Now, therefore don't content yourselves to live in darkness any longer.

Consider wisely what is best for yourselves, and take that course that will tend most for your good and the good of your children.

Religion is the greatest concern of mankind. The temporal concerns that they treat with you about at Albany from year to year are mere childish trifles in comparison of this.

For by and by you must all die and go into another world, and then none of the things of this world will do you any good. But the things of religion, in their effects and consequences, last forever.

When you are dead, your eyes will be open. Then this world will look little to you, and you shall know that religion is infinitely the greatest concern.

'Tis because men are blind that they are not more concerned for the god of their souls and the souls of their poor children.

'Tis because they are blind that they go into drunkenness and spend away their lives in wickedness.

The devil blinds men's eyes and tries to his utmost to keep 'em in the dark, that he may destroy 'em.

I have read of some nations, that when they take children captives in war, they keep 'em well for a while and feed 'em with the best till they are fat, and then kill 'em and eat 'em.

So the devil does by wicked men.

Now, therefore, look well about you and consider what is best for yourselves and your children.

There never was such an opportunity for you to be brought into the light as there is now.

We invite you to come and enjoy the light of the Word of God, which is ten thousand times better that [the] light of the sun.

There is such a thing as this light's shining into the heart, as it does into the hearts of all good men.

And when it does so, it changes their hearts and makes 'em like to Jesus Christ.

'Tis as when you hold a glass out in the light of the sun, the glass will shine with a resemblance of the sun's brightness.

Like a sweet and beautiful flower in the spring.

Before the heart of a man is sanctified, the heart won't receive the light of the Word of God.

A wicked man that hears the Word of God and won't receive it is like a piece of dung in the light of the sun. It sends forth a stink, but reflects no light.

When the light of God's Word shines into the heart, it gives new life to the soul.

You see how it is [in] the spring. When the sun shines on the earth and trees, it gives 'em new life, makes the earth look green. It causes flowers to appear and give a good smell.

So it is in the heart of a man when the light of God's Word shines into it.

Wisdom and knowledge in religion is better than silver or gold and all the riches of the world.

The light, when it shines into the heart, is sweeter than the honey, and the gospel will be a pleasant sound to you when you come to understand it.

Therefore if you would be a wise and a happy people, put yourselves in the way of receiving this light.

You love your children: therefore take care for their instruction, that they may be the children of the light, the children of God, and not the children of the devil.

If you never have this light shine into the heart, you must dwell forever in darkness, in another world, with the devil, the prince of darkness, in hell.

And there is burning heat but no light.

But if you receive this light into your hearts, you will be prepared to die and fitted to dwell in heaven, which is a world of light. And there you yourselves will shine forever forth as the sun in the kingdom of Jesus Christ.

In this sermon, Edwards opts for a basic presentation of the gospel and repeatedly uses light and darkness metaphors to illustrate the contrast between those who know God and those who are evil. "Now those nations that have the Scripture, they enjoy light ... But the nations that have not the Bible live in great darkness, and the devil, the prince of darkness, reigns over 'em." Edwards is quick to lay the blame for the Indians' lack of knowledge of salvation at the feet of the English settlers, who failed to teach the Indians how to read so they could study the Bible for themselves. He states "Your forefathers have for a great many ages lived in great darkness. And since the white people came over the seas and have settled in these parts of the world, they have not done their duty to you. They have greatly neglected you." Here Edwards is no doubt thinking back to Solomon Stoddard's sermon, "Question whether God is not Angry with the Country for doing so little towards the Conversion of the Indians?" when he says, "This has been shameful neglect of the white people, by which the great God has undoubtedly been made very angry." He speaks openly of how the

French have not only kept the Indians from learning to read the Bible on their own, but also have been preaching a distorted and false religion to them. "When the Bible is hid from 'em, they can cheat 'em and make 'em believe what they have a mind to."

Edwards is quick to point out that the English have been no better in their treatment of the Indians and that some English among them, who were not true Christians, were even taking advantage of them: "And many of the English and Dutch are against your being instructed. They choose to keep you in the dark for the sake of making a gain of you. For as long as they keep you in ignorance, 'tis more easy to cheat you in trading with you." While Edwards no doubt felt that the English were more civilized and that part of his duty was to instruct the Indians in proper societal as well as spiritual living, he is also quick to remind everyone of their equal standing before a holy God. He points out that the only difference between the English and the Indians is that God had given the English the truth of Scripture first, rendering them duty-bound to share it with the Indians. "We are no better than you in no respect, only as God had made us to differ and has been pleased to give us more light. And now we are willing to give it to you." He summarizes by discoursing at length on the contrast between light and dark and implores them to come to the light that is "ten thousand times brighter than [the] light of the sun." He concludes by encouraging them to teach their children the truth of Scripture, saying, "You love your children: therefore take care for their instruction, that they may be children of the light, the children of God, and not the children of the devil."

Sermon to the Stockbridge Indians–August, 1751

After a few months preaching to the Mohicans, Edwards seems to have altered his presentation style, foregoing a narrative description of the passage at the beginning in exchange for immediate exposition. We see that he also has changed from a salvation message to a Christian living focus and becomes more emphatic and descriptive in his language about hell and the eternal damnation of the lost.

SERMON TO THE STOCKBRIDGE INDIANS
August, 1751[7]

2 Corinthians 4:18
While we look not at the things which are seen, but at the things which are not seen: for the things which are seen are temporal; but the things which are not seen are eternal.

By the things are seen are meant The Things of this world & by the things which are not seen are meant the Things of another world. all the Things of this world are but for a Time & will come to an End.

So it is with all that men have here all their Riches & honours & Pleasures. These things are often times taken away from men while They Live. But men don't lose these Things while They live yet they can last no longer than their Lives and life we see lasts but a little while. The Time soon comes when men die & return to dust.

Death reaches all souls of men little & Great. rich & poor. All alike go down to the Grave. And when the die they can carry nothing away with Them of the all that They have enjoyed in this world. And the world itself will at last come to an end.

The Time is coming when this Earth with all the cities & Kingdoms that are upon it shall be burnt up. And when the sun shall cease to Go round & shall leave off shining. And there shall be no more sun moon nor stars

But there is another world that now is not seen. & the Things of that have no End. There is a world of Happiness where Christ is & where the Angels are & where all Good men shall be. And there is a world of misery which is a Place appointed for devils & wicked men.

Tho The Things of another world are not seen yet tis certain there is such a world.

---

[7] This transcription is numbered 1001 at the Jonathan Edwards Center at Yale.

For the Great God that governs the world is a just & righteous God & he will see to it that wicked men shall be punished & good men Rewarded. But we see 'tis not so in this world. Here all things come alike to all. Sometimes wicked men greatly Prosper in this world & good men meet with great sorrow & trouble. Sometimes in this world some of the worst of men are great Kings.

And some of the best of men have been cruelly treated by wicked men and could have no relief in this world. There have been a great many Good men that have been persecuted by wicked men & have been put to cruel & tormenting deaths for their Religion. Doubtless therefore there is another world wherein will do justice & where Good men shall be happy & wicked men miserable.

God suffers wicked men to Prosper & good men to be afflicted here because he Knows the Times of that Life is short and another world is coming where all Things shall be set to rights.

And God had told us plainly in his word that there is another world & has told us how he will dispose of Good & Bad there. And as God has told us that there is another world so he has told us that the Things of another world are everlasting.

Men[']s Bodies will die but their souls will never die. And at the End of the world their bodies will rise & their souls will unite into their bodies again. And then men will never die any more but both soul & Body will remain forever. Nor will mens state & condition be ever changed after death But they then [that] are happy will be Happy forever & They that are miserable will be miserable forever.

Heaven is a world where there are no such Changes as there are in this world. In this world all things are Changeable. A man may be one day Rich & another day poor. [One] day a King. & another day a poor person. One day in Health & another day sick. One day a Conquerour in war and another day a poor captive. One day alive & strong & another day dead.

Like the Grass that in the morning is green & flourishing but before night is cut down withered. But the saints in Heaven shall be above the Reach of all such Changes. There will be life forever & no more death. There shall be health & [no] more sickness. Peace & no war. There shall be Love & Friendships & no Enemies. Joy & Pleasure & no more sorrow or Pain. Joyful singing & no more groaning or weeping.

And on the other Hand as to them that Go to Hell. That they must be forever that shall never come out. They shall be cast into a furnace of fire. Which is a fire that never will be quenched & never will go out.

When men in this world are thrown into a fire They quickly die & the fire burns 'em up & then They feel the Pain no more. But in the fire of Hell the wicked shall never be burnt up & shall never die. Not only will their souls be in Hell but their Bodies shall be cast into Hell fire after the End of the world when their Bodies shall be raised again. And then their Bodies will be as full of fire within & without as ever a red hot iron was in the midst of a fierce fire. Their Heads & their Brains & all their flesh & Bones shall be full of fire & yet They shall never die. Their souls wont be burned by the fire but shall have quick feeling to feel torment forever.

Now therefore that is the Counsel that I give you. Do as the apostle did. Don't look at the Things which are see —But—

Don't Let your mind be taken up about the Things of this world. You all of you know you must die in a little Time & leave all these Things for ever. And why will you mind that which is but for a moment more than that which lasts forever.

You would think he was a fool that should prefer the pleasure of one Hour to the Comfort & Happiness many years. But if a man could live in that world a Thousand years that is less in comparison of eternity, then the Twinkling of an Eye is to a mans whole Life. Is it not more to be desired to be rich & happy a Thousand years then for one minute.

Consider seriously what Eternity is that without any End. It is that which can't be numbered or counted. If a man should spend a Thousand years in doing nothing also but counting & reckoning he could not come to the End of it. He could do nothing towards it. He would be no more to the End of it after He had spent all that Time in Reading then at the beginning.

If we reckon as many years as there are leaves on all the trees in the world or as many as there are drops of Rain that fall on the Face ever since the world of the Earth begun that is nothing to Eternity.

If the whole ocean was to be dry by taking away one drop at a time and but one drop was to be taken away in a Thousand years till it was all Gone, it would be a long time before the sea would be dry.

But this Long time long as it is nothing to Eternity.

How long a Time then is this for a man to lie burning in Hell. It would be a dreadful Thing to lie all over the in fire of a great oven like a burning Coal one Quarter of an hour. More dreadful to bear this a whole day as a whole year. O then how dreadful to bear this. What can we suppose They think of it that are gone to Hell that feel this misery.

When They feel this misery & look forward and consider that this is the misery that is to last forever & ever & never is to have an End how does it seem to em. They seek death but cannot find it. They desire to die but death shall flee from 'em. They find none to pity and help 'em. If They cry to God to pity 'em and deliver 'em he will not do it. For its too late.

They should have hearkened to God in their Lifetime. Then God called to them & They would not hear & now therefore when They call to Him He will not hear. They wish they never had been born. They wish They might be turned into a toad or snake for This They will Know will be better than to lie from in that misery.

When They Think of lying there thousands & ten thousands of years & then think that there will be no End. Oh how will their Hearts sink.

Eternity don't appear to Them as it does to wicked men in this world. Wicked men here make Light of it and bent much affected with the thought of it but it is not so with Them.

There are some that have been in Hell already above 4000 years & have not had one moments rest all This while. How do you think it makes them feel to consider that They are no nearer to an End then They were at first.

I don't tell you these things to trouble and afflict you but I tell you Them to warn you that so you mayn't come to this Place of Torment.

You had better hear of Hell fire now then feel it hereafter. Better now be in great distress of mind about it.

Sinners need to be waked out of their sleep & to be greatly concerned & afraid that now They may forsake their sins & escape Hell.

That is one Reason why so many Go to hell That They think no more of & are no more concerned about it while there is opportunity to Escape.

You had need to be concerned about these things for there are but few that are saved. The world is full of people & men are dying continually. It may be there is not one minute but that some body or other dies. And most of 'em Go to Hell. There are but few that go to Heaven.

There are but few Good. It is a great thing to be a truly good man. In order to be a good man, must have new heart. They must be born again & become new men.

You had need to make Haste for the work is great that you have to do in order to your Going to Heaven. Don't put it off till you come to lie on a sick bed. It may then it will be too late.

Some wicked when They come to die have died in dreadfull horror & distress. Some men on a deathbed have cried out world, Eternity, Eternity. And some have said. World I would give a thousand worlds that I might live a little longer. To have a little more opportunity to make my Peace with God.

You are all made for Eternity.

Consider your time is short. The Opportunity you have to get an interest in Christ will soon be gone. God has appointed the time---set your hands that you cannot Pass.

Consider how much of your life is gone already. Uncertainty of life.

If may you say with in your self I am now well in Health. Now Time enough hereafter for me to think for these Things & become a good man. But you will be fools to run the venture of it.

Death commonly comes unexpectedly. While men are putting off & thinking They shall have time enough then death comes suddenly upon it & they bent prepared & be this means multitudes go to Hell. They set their Hearts on Things of this world. Those things are mortal.

You must not look at Things which are seen, must not set your Hearts on the Things of this World but the Things of another world. You must forever forsake all drunkenness & all Lying & all malice & all stealing & cheating & every other way of wickedness.

Hell is full of drunkards & Lyars & malicious Persons.

Strictly keep the sabbath day & pray to God every day morning & night. And pray to God to give light in your minds. Know him. Trust in Christ Love God above all. Love all men. Walk in all God's ways. That you must be if you are the Children of God. The Children of God are holy Persons.

Tis a great mercy that God has told us how we may escape Hell & be happy in another world. Some sin in darkness & never Hear any Thing about it. Great mercy that you hear. Great mercy that you are not in Hell.

Men that had Good opportunities once & would not improve 'em are now in Hell. If They now Cry what a fool was I that I would now hearken to Counsel.

Now hearken to me this day then you will Rejoyce here after. Bless God forever that ever you heard this sermon.

Here it may be some will ask why God would inflict so great a Punishment. Answer God is infinitely great. Infinitely holy. Sin is infinitely bad.

By August of 1751, the time when Edwards preached this sermon, he had been with the Mohicans just over six months. During that time, he had been getting acquainted with his congregation and had been establishing a correspondence with English government officials over issues he observed in the Stockbridge settlement. Here, he chose 2 Corinthians 4:18, and from the foundation of these few words, builds his whole message. Having had a few months to get to know where his people are at spiritually, he changes from gently teaching them about salvation through Christ, to a hard-hitting reality check of the outcome should they not embrace God's gift of salvation immediately. This sermon is very reminiscent of "Sinners in the Hands of an Angry God," and there is a strong sense of urgency as he tells them, "Death commonly comes unexpectedly. While men are putting off & thinking. They shall have enough time then death comes suddenly."

The point of his discourse is to demonstrate the brevity of human days and the futility of putting emphasis and effort into transitory possessions, rather than a focusing on eternity. Though people pile up riches and seek honor among their fellow men, Edwards reminds them that such endeavours are fleeting and can be quickly taken from them. But even if they are not, he reminds them, "But [if] men don't lose these Things while They live yet they can last no longer than their Lives." None of what they accumulate or accomplish during life will accompany them after death. He also reminds them that a time is coming when even the earth itself will pass away, and when "all the cities & Kingdoms that are upon it shall be burnt up."

He then moves to a consideration of the contrasts between the two-world system of heaven and hell, saying, "There is a world of Happiness where Christ is … & there is a world of misery which is a place appointed for devils and wicked men." He acknowledges that often in this life the wicked prosper and good men suffer ill, but also assures them that ultimately all will come to a reckoning under God's judgement. He moves to the transitory nature of this life and draws from Matthew 6:30,[8] "Wherefore, if God so clothe the grass of the field, which to day is, and to morrow is cast into the oven, shall he not much more clothe you, O ye of little faith?"; Isaiah 40:8, "The grass withereth, the flower fadeth: but the word of our God shall stand for ever.", and 1 Peter 1:24–25, "For all flesh is as grass, and all the glory of man as the flower of grass. The grass withereth, and the flower thereof

---

[8] All Scripture references in discussing Edwards' sermons will be taken from the KJV since that is the version he would have used.

falleth away: But the word of the Lord endureth for ever. And this is the word which by the gospel is preached unto you." He states, "Like the Grass that in the morning is green & flourishing but before night is cut down withered."

He then reminds them that the righteous before God need not be concerned with the brevity of life, and tells them they will enjoy an eternity of happiness and bliss in God's presence: "But the saints in Heaven shall be above the Reach of all such Changes. Joy & Pleasure & no more sorrow or Pain. Joyful singing & no more groaning or weeping."

Next, Edwards turns to the contrasting state of those who do not embrace God's gift of salvation: "On the other Hand ... They shall be cast into a Furnace of Fire which is a fire that never will be quenched & never will go out." Perhaps his emphasis here on the unquenchable fire is a reference to one of the most important roles in the tribe—that of the fire keeper, whose responsibility it was to ensure the tribes' fire never went out; to allow such a thing to happen would have been to betray the sacred role entrusted to them. Edwards goes on to describe what happens when the human body is thrust into a fire; namely, that as the body is consumed by flames, death soon follows. Not so with those who are destined to suffer an eternity in Hell, however. In the most graphic of terms he attempts to shock them into the realization of the severity of such an eternal punishment, stating, "Their heads, their Brains, their Hearts & Bowels & all their flesh & Bones shall be full of fire & yet They shall never die ... but shall have quick feeling to feel torment forever."

Edwards moves on to practical counsel on how to avoid such a terrible fate as eternal suffering. He tells them not to be concerned with temporal things but to place their interest in things which will endure forever. He then attempts to give the Indians an idea of what eternity is by providing them with a number of illustrations and analogies. For example, he states that "If the whole ocean was to be dry by taking away one single drop at a time and but one drop was to be taken away in a Thousand years till it was all gone, it would be a long time before the sea would be dry. But this Long time long as it is nothing to Eternity." In response, Edwards demonstrates his care and concern for them by suggesting a practical solution to the dilemma of hell. "I don't tell you these things to trouble and afflict you but I tell you Them to warn you that so you mayn't come to this Place of Torment." He says that it is better for them to know about the severity of the impending punishment of sinners before it is too late. He informs them that most people won't receive such warnings, and that many will continue on their way without giving the matter any thought. He implores his hearers, however, to become good men by giving their heart to Christ and being born again. "In order to be a good man must have [a] new heart. They must be born again." He reminds them of the urgency of this decision, for time is passing and their own death could be at any moment. "Death commonly comes unexpectedly, while men are putting off & thinking they shall have time enough. Then death comes suddenly upon it & they ben't [be] prepared."

As he comes to the end of his sermon, he confronts them once more with the various sins plaguing the Mohicans: "You must forever forsake all drunkenness & all Lying & all malice & all stealing & Cheating & every other way of wickedness." He then calls them to repent and live holy lives, giving up those things which are seriously impeding their physical and spiritual lives. He tells them that they are fortunate to have heard this message for there are many who, having rejected it, now suffer in eternal torment. He concludes with a rhetorical question that may have been on some Indians' minds: "Here it may be some will ask why God would inflict so great a punishment. Answer God is infinitely great, Infinitely Holy. Sin is infinitely bad." He closes with the ultimate truth of reality—whereas almighty God is the epitome of good; sin is the epitome of evil.

In 1754, as he entered the middle years of his tenure with the Mohicans, it was to be a time of severe trial both for Edwards personally, but also for the Stockbridge community. To begin with, he was constantly in conflict with the Williams family and battling over the situation at the school being run by Ephraim Williams and Captain Martin

Kellogg. It was becoming clear that not only were the children's studies being neglected, but the money was also being siphoned off for non-school related purposes; the boys were also being sent to work the fields rather than attend their classes.

There was also the constant stress of living under threat of potential war with the French and Indians from Canada, who had been making sorties into the area. Eventually, in 1754, Edwards became ill for about six months and was unable to carry on his pastoral duties. Marsden states, "If his long illness involved despondency, there was much to be despondent about. The mission school was in pathetic condition, war seemed inevitable and the survival of any English in Stockbridge was an open question."[9]

Another incident also occurred in the fall of that year which set everyone on edge and put the settlers into a panic. On September 1, 1754, a parishioner, late for service, ran in and told of a massacre that had occurred close by. Frazier gives the account. "Passing the cabin of Samuel Brown's son-in-law, he had seen an Indian dragging a child outside, and gave chase. When the abductor saw the man pursuing him, he tomahawked the child and fled. Returning to the cabin, the churchgoer found a servant and an infant dead and the father and two other children cowering under a bed."[10] When Edwards appealed to the authorities for assistance, soldiers came into the area and a stockade was built around his house. This added additional stress to Edwards as he was responsible for the billeting and feeding of the soldiers while they were erecting the stockade. "In October, the expenses of such hospitality became crushing, and he was obliged to cry to the General Court for mercy. He had provided "800 meals of victuals, pasturing 150 horses, and 7 gallons of good west Indian rum" as well as food for "all poor

---

[9] George M. Marsden, *Jonathan Edwards A Life* (New Haven: Yale University Press, 2003), 410.

[10] Frazier, *The Mohicans*, 107.

people driven from their homes above thro' fear."[11] Edwards, however, being their spiritual leader, was forced to overcome his own afflictions and look to those under his care. Ultimately, Edwards returned to the pulpit.

We will now look at two sermons he preached in March of 1755. What will immediately become apparent is that he was obviously deeply affected by what was happening around him. His outlines also become much more abbreviated, likely due to the fact that he was still not a well man at this time; not to mention a house full of soldiers, his continuing battle with the Williams family, and the French and Indian war. His daughter, Esther, had come for a visit and recorded the circumstances under which they were living. Frazier tells us,

> At her father's fortified home she confessed on one of her several sleepless September nights, "Almost overcome with fear, last night and Thursday night we had a watch at this fort and most of the Indians came to lodge here. Some thought that they heard the enemy last night. ... O how distressing to live in fear every moment."[12]

Be that as it may, Edwards knew his duty, and continued to prepare and deliver poignant and powerful sermons.

Sermon to the Stockbridge Indians–March 5, 1755

With war threatening the frontier in early March 1755, Edwards chooses an Old Testament passage to bring the Stockbridge Indians a sense of hope and encouragement. His doctrinal statement from the text is simple and shows his Calvinist leanings—regardless of the circumstances, be they a time of peace or a time of war, all events occur because almighty God wills them to be. He then proceeds to elucidate four main points.

---

[11] Sarah Cabot Sedgwick and Christina Sedgwick Marquand, *Stockbridge 1739-1939: A Chronicle* (Great Barrington, MA.: The Berkshire Courier, 1939), 75.

[12] Frazier, *The Mohicans*, 121.

[TO THE] STOCKBRIDGE INDIANS "PRIVATE FAST FOR OUR DEFENCE FROM THE ENEMY, MARCH 5, 1755"[13]

2 Chronicles 20:6
And said, O Lord God of our fathers, art not thou God in heaven? and rulest not thou over all the kingdoms of the heathen? and in thine hand is there not power and might, so that none is able to withstand thee?

[DOCTRINE.]
[God orders things] just as he pleases. And all defence and success in war is from him

I. In a Time of war, he sees and knows all things concerning the affair. [God] knows who is in the right. [There is] always one side in the wrong. [God knows] what it is that moves 'em, whether good principles [or bad]. [God knows] all the designs of the enemy [Their] plots. The things] they keep secret. Knows all that They do. Sees in darkness. Sees all the hiding places in the minds. All under the whole Heaven. Knows when a People are most in danger. Never sleeps.

II. God's wisdom is above all that cunning and craftiness that men use in a time of war. Many are very subtil and Crafty. Are[14] very cunning in their schemes and plots for the carrying on the war. By their craftiness, they often deceive others & lead 'em into a snare. Sometimes a nation in a time of war have very cunning rulers and great men. [The] take Counsel. Use all their cunning. But God is wiser. They are as little children and fools. [God] knows how to disappoint. [God knows how to] lead 'em into the Pits they have digged for others. Men have no wisdom or understanding but what God has given 'em. Makes wiser than the beasts.[15] Makes some men wiser than others.

---

[13] This transcription is numbered 1133 at the Jonathan Edwards Center at Yale.
[14] MS: "have."
[15] MS: "beat."

III. Sometimes the devil leads men to make war

[The devil is] cunninger than men. God's wisdom is above. God's strength is above the strength of men. [Above the] strongest men. The greatest armies. All their strength put together. [God] gave 'em their strength. Men are but little worms. All nations before him are as nothing. [The]strongest armies as Chaff before a strong wind. As dry straw before devouring Fire. God made the world. Manages the sun moon & stars. Manages the sea. Can shake the world in Pieces.

IV. God has all Things in his Hands. All nations. All Kings. Made every man, body & soul, and all are his. The greatest nations and armies as much in his power as one little child. Their Hearts [are in his hands]. He can turn them. He directs all their thoughts. Lead to right thoughts. Armies by land & ships at sea [are in God's hands]. [The] weather [is] of his ordering. [God can] sink their ship. Their Hearts are in his Hands. Give courage. Direct their thought in the time of the fight. Can make 'em disagree one with another. Has men's health in his[16] hands.

With war threatening the frontier in early March 1755, Edwards chooses an Old Testament passage to bring the Stockbridge Indians a sense of hope and encouragement. His doctrinal statement from the text is simple and shows his Calvinist leanings—regardless of the circumstances, be they a time of peace or a time of war, all events occur because almighty God wills them to be. He then proceeds to elucidate four main points.

His first point is that even though war seems imminent, God is omniscient, and "sees and knows all thing[s] concerning the affair." He also reminds them that though there will always be those who are right, and those who are wrong, God can distinguish them from each other because he perceives the intent of our hearts. He mentions that while the enemy may have intelligent and clever leaders, compared to the wisdom of God, "They are as little children and fools." Here he refers to Proverbs 26:27, "Whoso diggeth a pit shall fall therein: and he

---

[16] MS: "their."

that rolleth a stone, it will return upon him," and says, "[God will] lead 'em into the Pits they have digged for others." He repeatedly uses the terms "crafty" and "cunning" with regards to the schemes and plans of their enemies, and Edwards stresses that all man's intelligence is a gift from the creator: "Men have no wisdom or understanding but what God has given 'em."

In his third point, Edwards introduces them to Satan, the author of all wars, and states that, "Sometimes the devil leads men to make war." Satan loves to see God's creation in discord and because he is "cunninger than men," often deceives men into conflicts with one another in an effort to keep them from God. Edwards demonstrates the ultimate futility of Satan's schemes since "God's wisdom is above," and he already knows what Satan has planned. He also describes the futility of men's demonstrations of power and, in classic Puritan style, describes humanity from God's perspective, namely, that "men are but little worms. All nations before him are as nothing." Not only God can blow all the armies away "as chaff before a strong wind" but the ultimate end of wicked men is "as dry straw before devouring fire."

In his fourth and final point he brings them back to reassurance and comfort, and exhorts them to put their trust in God, for "God has all things in his hands." If almighty God is in control of all people, then there is nothing that can happen to them that is not already within the providential will of God; and God will certainly "give courage [and] direct their thought in the time of the fight."

Sermon to the Stockbridge Indians–March, 1755

This is yet another martial sermon to the Stockbridge Indians, who fought on the English side against the French and their Indian allies in the Seven Years' War.

Stockbridge Indians–March 1755[17]

---

[17] This transcription is numbered 1134 at the Jonathan Edwards Center at Yale.

LIVE SO THAT YOU NEED NOT BE AFRAID TO DIE

Ecclesiastes 8:8.
There is no man that hath power over the spirit to retain the spirit; neither hath he power in the day of death: and there is no discharge in that war; neither shall wickedness deliver those that are given to it.

I. Most men are very much afraid of death.

II. When death appears near, then especially are most men unwilling to die. When they come to see the enemy, and look him in the face.

III. Wicked very often are dreadfully afraid of death, when they see they are like to die. Reason.

IV. But yet, there is no avoiding death. All men must die. Former generations, most of 'em [were] afraid of death. Wicked men in former times.

V. All men must go at the time appointed. Can't stay any longer.

VI. Wickedness will not deliver 'em.

[APPLICATION.]

Live so that you need not be afraid to die. Seeing there is no discharge. Seeing {all must die}.

Some men have no cause [to be afraid]. Many men have got above the fears of death. Been very willing to die.

Don't live so as to make death terrible. How. But to make it your friend. How.

First thing is to consider. You will have your eyes open. How miserable you will be, if you live and die in your sin.

Consider the warning God has lately given you.[18] If you should die senseless, what good will that do you.

---

[18] Possibly referring generally to the outbreak of the French & Indian War, or to the raid by Schaghticoke Indians in Sept, 1975 that resulted in the killing of four Stockbridge residents.

In this sermon, Edwards' points are clipped, with no development, and there is a definite sense of urgency to his outline, as if even some in his native audience are about to join the fighting. Without naming a formal doctrine, he gives six brief headings and then moves to an equally brief and direct application, both of which deal with how to rise above the "fears of death" and even to make death one's "friend."

Edwards' main headings are a series of undeveloped assertions. He commences with the truism that all people are afraid to die, and that the closer one comes to death, the greater the fear. He also states that the wicked are more afraid when they see death approaching and that, at the time of death, their "Wickedness will not deliver 'em." There will be no way for them to outsmart God and avoid death.

His application is likewise outlined and lacks any explicit direction. His initial statement, however, is clear enough: "Live so that you need not be afraid to die." Further Edwards encourages them, "Don't live so as to make death terrible," but rather so as "to make it your friend." Both of these are followed with a cryptic "How," but Edwards' specific counsels on these points must remain speculative. His conclusion is terse and stark, and he tells them that if they continue to live sinful lives and die in such a state, it will be miserable for them. He reminds them that their present situation is unstable, and events that had happened around Stockbridge should provide them with an ample warning to be spiritually prepared for the possibility of death. His notes end abruptly: "If you should die senseless, what good will that do you." Essentially, he is saying that if they died without having lived not afraid of death, then they must surely face eternal peril.

Edwards' first point is a statement of truth, and simply states that people are afraid to die. While some are afraid of the exact manner of their death, most fear what will happen to them after they die. His second point builds on the first, and that is that the closer one comes to death, the greater the fear. His third point indicates that the wicked are more afraid when they see death approaching. He does not here expand on the reason why, but we can speculate that he was referring to the certainty that all will be judged after death and be called to account for how they have conducted themselves during their lives. He would probably also have reminded them that they would also be faced with an eternity separated from God, and subjected to eternal punishment in hell. He might have alluded to any number of passages to support his point, most particularly Hebrews 9:27, "And as it is appointed unto men once to die, but after this the judgment."

His fourth point is clear and concise—everyone dies and no one can avoid it, and stresses that throughout all generations people have feared their impending death. His fifth point is that no one has any control over when they will die, and that God has determined a person's life span and "All men must Go at the Time appointed." In this thought, Edwards is drawing on Job 14:5, "Seeing his days are determined, the number of his months are with thee, thou hast appointed his bounds that he cannot pass." The sixth point, with which he ends the doctrinal portion of his sermon, has an interesting slant. He reminds his hearers that at the time of death "wickedness will not deliver 'em." It will not be possible for anyone to outwit God and cheat death by using any worldly schemes.

Again, his application is cryptic and lacks any real direction. His clear statements are that they should "live so that you need not be afraid to die" and here would presumably have taught them how to live a holy, Christ-like life. He would probably have alluded to Galatians 5:22, 23, "But the fruit of the Spirit is love, joy, peace, longsuffering, gentleness, goodness, faith, meekness, temperance: against such there is no law." He assures them that there are many who, in living a godly life, "got above the fears of death," and have even, "been very willing to die." Edwards knew there had been martyrs throughout the ages who had voluntarily chosen to die, beginning with Christ himself, who would also die for those who would come to God through him. Edwards may also have thought of more recent occurrences. Just 200 years earlier under the reign of Mary I, Puritan ministers Hugh Latimer (1487– 16 October 1555), bishop of Worcester, England, and Nicholas Ridley (1500–16 October 1555), Bishop of London were burned at the stake outside Balliol College, Oxford. As the fire was lit, Latimer said to Ridley, "Play the man, Master Ridley; we shall this day light such a candle, by God's grace, in England, as I trust shall never be put out."[19] Edwards himself was a product of that Puritan movement and would have acknowledged the grace of God that would sustain believers in the severest of trials.

His second application is to encourage them to live so that they need not fear death. Again, the "How," in his outline is not fleshed out and so we must speculate as to how he would have instructed them. Since their situation is such that there is the ever-present threat from those who may attack and kill them, he no doubt would have taken them to Matthew 10:28, "And fear not them which kill the body, but are not able to kill the soul: but rather fear him which is able to destroy both soul and body in hell." He may also have taken them to 1 Corinthians 15:54–55, "So when this corruptible shall have put on incorruption, and this mortal shall have put on immortality, then shall be brought to pass the saying that is written, Death is swallowed up in victory. O death, where is thy sting? O grave, where is thy victory?"

He tells them they must remember that God is in control and alone will determine the manner and time of their death. If they are his children, they need not be fearful of death, and that they should make death their friend. Once more the "How," is not given, yet he tells them that they will have their eyes opened. We can be confident that he would likely have referred to passages such as 1 Corinthians 12:13, "For now we see through a glass, darkly; but then face to face: now I know in part; but then shall I know even as also I am known." And since he is constantly reminding them that Satan is the enemy of their souls, he might have turned to Hebrews 2:14–15, "Since the children have flesh and blood, [Jesus] too shared in their humanity so that by his death he might break the power of him who holds the power of death—that is, the

---

[19] W. Grinton Berry, M.A., *Foxe's Book of Martyrs* (London: The Religious Tract Society, n.d.), 309.

devil— and free those who all their lives were held in slavery by their fear of death."

In conclusion, he tells them that if they continue to live sinful lives and die in such a state, how miserable it will be for them. He says, "Consider the warning God has lately given you." Edwards is reminding them that the present situation is unstable and that the recent massacre close to Stockbridge should provide an ample warning to them to be prepared spiritually for the possibility of death. His notes end abruptly: "If you should die senseless what Good will that do you." If they die without having embraced the salvation God has offered them, through Christ, then their lives will have counted for nothing and their death will be pointless. Since Edwards did not leave us any complete notes, we do not have the benefit of knowing if this was his concluding statement to them.

As we move to Edwards' farewell sermons it is important to be reminded of his reason for leaving the Stockbridge Mohicans. Edwards' son-in-law, Aaron Burr Sr., the second president of Princeton University, died on September 24, 1757, at the age of forty-one. In the ensuing months the Board negotiated with Edwards to assume the role and become Burr's replacement. After a considerable amount of personal reticence over his suitability for the post, Edwards finally agreed. He arrived in Princeton in late January 1758, and was installed on February 16. Sadly, he would die a month later. Prior to leaving Stockbridge he preached two farewell sermons in January 1758.[20]

Farewell sermon to the Stockbridge Indians–January 8, 1758
The first of Edwards' two farewell sermons is a call for the Mohicans to remember those who have come to bring God's word to them.

GOD'S PEOPLE SHOULD REMEMBER

---

[20] These sermons were published in Wilson H. Kimnach, ed., *The Works of Jonathan Edwards* (New Haven: Yale University Press, 2006), 25:711–716. Used with permission of Yale University Press.

THEM THAT HAVE BEEN THEIR MINISTERS
January 8, 1758[21]

Hebrews 13:7-8
Remember them that have the rule over you, who have spoken to you the word of God: whose faith follow, considering the end of their conversation. Jesus Christ the same yesterday, and today, for forever.

[THREE PROPOSITIONS.]

I. *A people that have lived under the gospel should remember them that have been their ministers, who have spoken to 'em* the word of God. Remember how many [things have been done]: the words they have spoken, the pains they have taken, the prayers they have made, [and] whatever good examples they have set. [Remember] all the advantages they have had [under this ministry].

Reasons

[*First.*] They have been God's messengers. It is God's work they have been employed in. It is God's word that they have spoken to reveal God's mind. God's commands [have been taught] for God's glory. In remembering them, they remember God; in forgetting them, they forget God.

Second. Because the ministers that have spoken to them the word of God have labored for their greatest good. The word of God, which they have spoken, has been for their good. God gave his word for the sake of men, for their happiness. [They have brought 'em] the glorious gospel. They have taught 'em, counselled them, warned 'em, [and] shown 'em the way. Therefore, in remembering the ministers, they will remember themselves. [Never] forget themselves: it greatly concerns them to remember the things which they have spoken.

---

[21] This transcription is numbered 1177 at the Jonathan Edwards Center at Yale.

Third. God will remember, and call 'em to an account. Remember that they[22] may do [things] that they may report that they have made no better improvement [when] the next minister [comes here]. Come more to meeting. If ever it should be so that any talk against him and tell you he is good for nothing, don't mind them. Whether we shall ever see each other in this world is uncertain: but remember we must meet again at the last day.

II. *As ministers, if they are faithful, will come to an happy end at last, so will they also that follow their instructions.*

III. *A Christian people should comfort [themselves] that, though they may have many ministers, one after another, yet Jesus Christ, the great head of the church, is always the same.*

[APPLICATION.]

Remember how it has been with you: how much has been done for you. Remember the things I have told you:[23]

You that have gone on in drinking.

You that are professors of religion.

You that formerly [have] been of the church.

Young people.

You that have made it your care to live agreeable to the gospel.

As Edwards comes to the end of his tenure with the Mohicans, his final sermons to them are gentle and caring, suitably highlighting his role as their shepherd. In his previous two hundred sermons, preached since 1751, he presented the gospel in many ways. He taught them the truth

---

[22] Footnote in the transcript says, "Apparently meaning the enemies of the mission."

[23] Footnote in the transcript says, "JE had used the sheet out of which part of this sermon was made to construct a list of advantages and disadvantages of the Princeton position. The end of the "pros" continues to the bottom of this page, and "cons" begin on the next: not have much to say/ There can have books/ Trustees willing to favour me as to my studies/ Advantages to do good/ Prevent Evil/ [...] divert me [?] from study & writing.

of Scripture, and guided them as to proper living according to Biblical principles. Now, as his time with them is finished, he leaves them with a simple message: Don't forget me or the others who have given their lives to bring you the truth of God's Word.

He presents to them three reasons they should take heed to this message. First, the Indians should remember them because their ministers have been the very representatives of God to them. Second, their ministers have always labored for the Indians' highest good. And third, their ministers will be called to give an account of their work, and he warns them not to listen to idle talk or slander against their pastor. At this point, almost as if he knew he would never see them again, he tenderly reminds them, "but remember we must meet again at the last day." His second point is that faithful ministers, and their charges who remain faithful, will ultimately come to a peaceful and contented end. His final point is to remind them that although they may experience a number of ministers with differing personalities, customs and manners, their Lord, Jesus Christ, "the great head of the church, is always the same." In making this remark he may have referenced Hebrews 13:8, reminding them of "Jesus Christ the same yesterday, and to day, and for ever."

As he moves to the application portion of his message, he simply tells them to remember from where they have come and not to forget the effort that has been put forth on their behalf. One last time he pleads for them to stay on guard against alcohol—the one snare that has been their persistent challenge and downfall. He closes by calling all to live according to the call of the gospel.

Farewell sermon to the Stockbridge Indians–January 15, 1758
Edwards' second and final farewell sermon is a very short homily reminding the Mohicans to always be diligent.

Sermons

Watch and Pray Always–January 15, 1758[24]
Luke 21:36
Watch ye, and pray always.

I. Many dreadful things are coming upon this wicked world.

II. The righteous, and they only, shall be thought fit to escape those things that shall come.

III. All at last must be called to appear before Christ. Christ will come. All must see him. All must [be] brought before him.

IV. The righteous shall be thought worthy to stand before Christ and no others.

First. The righteous worthy.

Second. Wicked not worthy.[25]

V. We should watch and pray always that we may be thought worthy [to stand before Christ].

First. Watch.

Second. Pray.

Third. Always.

[APPLICATION.]

What must watch against. How watch. What need of watching. Always. Prayer. What pray for. How pray.

In his final discourse, Edwards gives an abbreviated message stressing the necessity for the Mohicans to be diligent in contact with God, who is their true source of strength, through prayer. Though by this time they had already lived through many agonizing and terrible experiences, Edwards warns them that it will get worse if they neglect the duty of prayer, reminding them that "Many dreadful things are coming

---

[24] This transcription is numbered 1178 at the Jonathan Edwards Center at Yale.

[25] Footnote in transcript says, "Upside down at the bottom of the first page is a list of Indian names made by JE: 'Chenequuge [?]/ Capt Checksonkum [?]/ Roberts wife/ Siah's wife/ Conokounts [?] wife.'"

upon this wicked world." He points out to them that only those who are in a right standing before God will escape the wrath that is to come and states that everyone, good and evil, will ultimately stand before the judgment seat of Christ. He perhaps would have here cited 2 Corinthians 5:9-10, "Therefore we make it our aim, whether present or absent, to be well pleasing to Him. For we must all appear before the judgment seat of Christ, that each one may receive the things done in the body, according to what he has done, whether good or bad." He assures them that only those who are in a right place with God will be found worthy and able to stand before Christ at the final judgment. The only way to be sure beyond doubt, he declared, is to always watch and pray.

As Edwards moves to the application portion of his sermon, he begins by describing to them the sorts of sins of which they should be aware, and the methods of how they should be diligent in fighting against them. Presumably he would have mentioned the importance of avoiding alcohol, as he had on so many other occasions. He would also most likely have given them practical instruction on avoiding becoming entrapped by those who would lead them to sin by encouraging them to stay in close fellowship with other believers. He wraps up his sermon by emphasizing the power of prayer and describes how to pray and what to pray for. We can only speculate what he would have counseled them to pray for, but we can guess he would have had them pray for strength to maintain their faith and diligence in times of trial, as well as for their leaders, and especially for the new minister which would soon be taking his place among them.

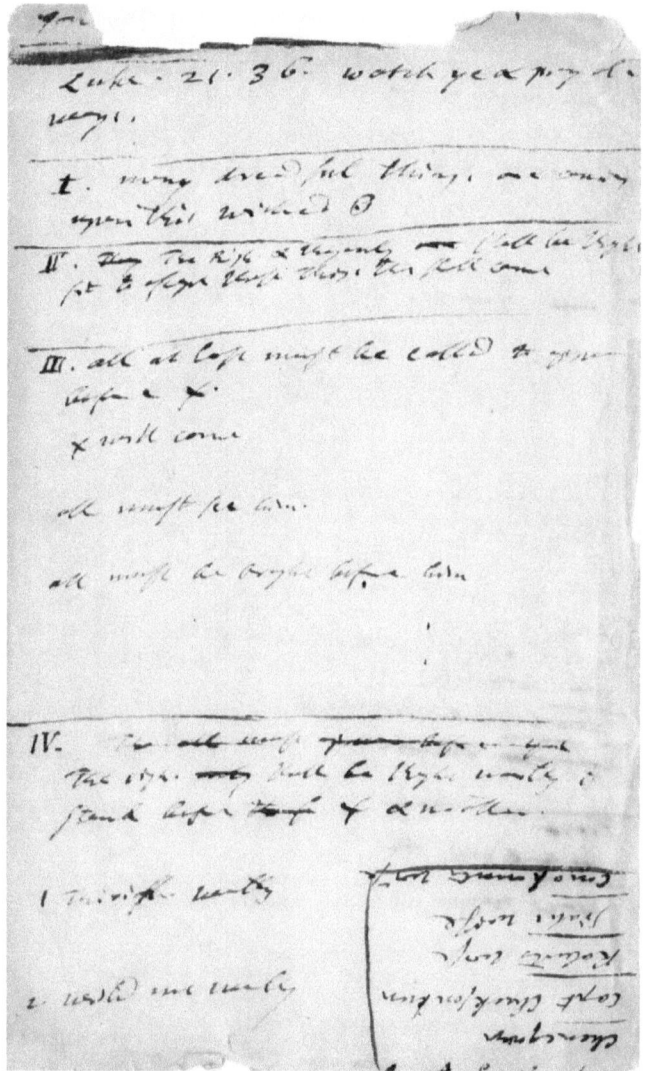

First page of Edwards' "Watch Ye & Pray Always" preached January 15, 1758. Beinecke Rare Book and Manuscript Library-Yale University

6

SUMMARY AND CONCLUSION

Throughout history, man's inhumanity to man has been a continual saga demonstrating the treachery that lies deeply embedded within the human heart. One of the most shocking examples of this inhumanity was the treatment of the indigenous American peoples at the hands of the Dutch and English settlers. But should that come as a surprise to us? After all, a disagreement between the very first two siblings ended in the death of one. When Cain was confronted by God regarding his brother's whereabouts, he responded, "I know not: Am I my brother's keeper?" (Genesis 4:9 KJV)

The corruption that resides within man is summed up in Jeremiah 17:9, "The heart is deceitful above all things, and desperately wicked: who can know it?" This verse shows us that evil inherently lives within our hearts. But not everyone used and abused the Indians. This study has shown that men such as Solomon and John Stoddard, John Sergeant, and Jonathan Edwards were but a few of the godly men who genuinely cared for the physical and spiritual well-being of the natives. While their motivation of "Christianizing by civilizing" the Indians may have been misguided, it came from an honest and sincere effort to do them good.

Jonathan Edwards came to the Mohicans of Stockbridge from a disappointing ministry in Northampton. He had assumed the role of pastor to a congregation deeply committed to the preaching and teaching of his iconic grandfather, Solomon Stoddard. Edwards was only twenty-six years old and disagreed with the "half-way covenant" that Stoddard had instituted in the church, and his own cousins were ringleaders in the decision that eventually saw him discharged. While the

Mohicans may have been happy to have a new minister after the untimely death of John Sergeant, many of the English settlers, as well as Edwards' own cousins from Northampton, opposed his appointment.

His preaching to the Mohicans and Mohawks was of a different style and the sermon content sometimes different from what he had preached in Northampton. As has been mentioned, Edwards was a master of rhetoric and the appropriate use of imagery to enhance his preaching and often drew analogies from nature that he recognized would speak to the Indians. The Mohicans were master storytellers and their history was largely drawn from illustrations related to nature. In referring to an early sermon Edwards preached to the Mohicans on Psalm 1:3, Wheeler says,

> Everything about Edwards' sermon suggests that he believed his new pastorate called for new methods of preaching and pastoring. The imagery of the sermon seems designed to resonate with the presumed sensibilities of his audience and with the rich, metaphorical cast of Indian rhetorical styles.[1]

Marsden concurs and states, "Edwards' sermons to the Indians reflect a good sense of his audience. He did not just preach simpler versions of his sermons to the English, which were almost all old Northampton sermons. Rather, consistent with his advice regarding Indian education, he picked themes that involved narratives and vivid metaphors."[2]

At the beginning of his ministry Edwards would consistently remind them of the particular sins that were plaguing them; specifically, drunkenness, lying and cheating. While he reminded them less of these vices in the ensuing years, he did return to them at his farewell sermon as a fatherly reminder. Like most English, he felt the Indians were un-

---

[1] Rachel Wheeler, *To Live Upon Hope* (Ithaca, New York: Cornell University Press, 2008), 185.

[2] George M. Marsden, *Jonathan Edwards A Life* (New Haven: Yale University Press, 2003), 393.

Summary and Conclusion

cultured and primitive in many ways, but he reminded them that despite their differences in culture they were all one in God's eyes. As Wheeler has noted,

> Edwards affirmed English cultural superiority, but he rejected any idea that this superiority was innate. Rather, he affirmed that the English had simply benefited from longer exposure to the gospel; so, Edwards informed the Indians, "we do no more than our duty in it for it was once with our Forefathers as 'tis with you." [3]

When one studies the sermons preached to the English, we see an obvious contrast in the balance of what Edwards preached. To the English, he stressed their obligations to God and referred more to the severity of punishment at the judgment. To the Mohicans, his sermons were of a gentler style and were more often directed at the mercy and love of God. He did not fail to speak plainly to the Indians about the suffering for those who rejected Christ, but it was of a lesser emphasis and repeated less often. Marsden affirms,

> Edwards did not shrink from preaching terror to the Indians or from explaining in narrative terms some hard points of Calvinism, such as original sin and the reasons for God's wrath and judgment, but he tempered these points with God's mercy as much as he could.[4]

It seems that Edwards was more temperate in his sermons to the Mohicans not only because he had compassion on them as their spiritual leader but because he also recognized how they were being manipulated and cheated by the settlers. To the end of his tenure with them, Edwards carried on a voluminous and relentless writing campaign to government officials on their behalf.

---

[3] Wheeler, *To Live*, 215.
[4] Marsden, *Jonathan Edwards*, 393.

Another sign of his care and concern for the Indians was the fact that unlike his predecessor, John Sergeant, Edwards built his home among the Mohicans. His children played with their children and his son; Jonathan Jr., also became fluent in their language. History indicates that Edwards was an imposing, distant individual, who spent much of his time studying and writing. This has led many to feel he was uncaring toward the Mohicans. While it is true that he produced his greatest theological works while in Stockbridge, it is equally true that he prepared and preached over 200 hundred sermons to them, as well as preaching to the white settlers and writing numerous letters for the Indians' welfare. Edwards had a difficult ministry from the outset. He was also plagued with constant criticism and conflict, which no doubt led to his bouts of severe illness. In spite of these trials, however, he was faithful to his calling to preach the gospel. Current scholarship is a testimony to the impact of his legacy as more has been written on Jonathan Edwards in this century than on almost any other theologian. Indeed, twenty-five percent of the articles in the most recent issue[5] of the Journal of the Evangelical Theological Society are devoted to a study of Jonathan Edwards' spirituality.

It has been said that the time Edwards spent in Stockbridge was the most rewarding time of his ministry. If the testimony of history is any indication, it may well have been, and surely led to a Christian legacy down to the modern day. In speaking with tribal member Mark Shaw, he stated emphatically,

> If it weren't for the ministry of Jonathan Edwards, my ancestors, my grandparents, my mother, and I would not be Christians today. There are five Christian churches on my small reservation. Jonathan Edwards and the other missionaries really changed the faith and beliefs of my Native American Nation.[6]

---

[5] *Journal of the Evangelical Theological Society*, La Mirada, CA, Volume 62, No. 3, September, 2019.

[6] Personal email from Mark Shaw, Tribal member, July 4, 2019.

Summary and Conclusion

Edwards' legacy lives on—but what about the Mohicans for whom he was so concerned? The United States government used various means to eliminate the Indians as a distinct people group including the Indian Removal Act of 1830 and the removal of their religious freedom in 1883. Various other efforts to have them relinquish their Indian identity and rights in exchange for US citizenship have also occurred. While attempts to steal Indian land and identity led to the demise of many of the indigenous tribes in the United States, the Mohicans have fought it every step of the way. Today this brave and proud people have maintained their unique identity and tribal status and continue to survive and thrive in Wisconsin. Here, they are slowly, but surely, regaining their lost lands. Their young people have embraced their heritage and culture, and there is a renewed effort to revive their language, which was almost lost. Today, as in the days of the mission to Stockbridge, there are many non-tribal members who support the Mohican history and work diligently for its preservation. Perhaps it is appropriate that we end this study with a prayer by Mohican tribal member Elaine M. Jacobi:

> We hear the voice of our Muh He Con Nuck people through the continually flowing waters, in the wind, the air, the plants, trees, animals and all humans.
>
> We are weak and need your strength and wisdom. We thank you for the renewing of Mother Earth, which gives us a promise of growth and newness.
>
> We ask you to help us as we pause and reflect upon our ancestors and early leaders. Our culture is not dead! Our ancestors of yesterday are still here in our people. We are all of creation and we are all related. Mother Nature and the natural laws have never changed. The sun, our Eldest Brother, still rises in the East, warms us and sets in the West. The moon, our Grandmother, controls the waters of the great oceans and her relationship to all the women of the world, shares responsibility for the birth of children. Everything we need for survival and substance is still here.

Our Mohican ancestors met Henry Hudson in view of the Catskill Mountains. They were far from being hostile, but kind and loving people. They had much interest in those strange visitors aboard the Half-Moon. The white visitors may have taken the fat of the land and everything else we hold dear to us, but above all we still have our Spirituality! When we were [are] spiritually connected, no one can ever take that away, except ourselves. For us as Mohican people we have our Language and Culture, our Talking Circles, our Legends and Traditions, our Helping Spirits, Sweat Lodges, Medicine Wheel, Social Dancing, Smudging rituals, and praying with the Eagle Feather. It was with great joy when our "Bibles" were used diligently as our ancestors journeyed Westward, to New York, then to Ohio, Indiana, Illinois, and Wisconsin. When crossing the swollen Illinois River, our people lost some of their possessions, but the "Bibles" in its Oaken Chest was preserved, and always placed on the alter[*sic*] wherever they settled in a new home and a new church. Putahmowus, help us as we rekindle the fires of these sacred values.

We ask Putahmowus for true healing, to help us turn to the values of our ancestors and acceptance to those who are different. We need the full strength of our community. The individual, family, and community are not separate. It calls for the power of the Creator, the wisdom of the warrior, and the heart of the Mother. It is a path of progress, not perfection.

We are looking in the wrong place when it comes to our culture. We need balance and harmony within ourselves. We need to do a personal inventory to put ourselves and our weaknesses before our Creator.

Putahmowus, Listen to your children praying,

Send your Spirit in this place,

Send us love, send us power, send us Grace! Aniishick! [Thank you][7]

---

[7] Mark Shaw, ed., *Reflections on the Waters That Are Never Still: A Literary Journal of the Mohican People* (Saline, MI: McNaughton & Gunn, 2015), 46–47.

Summary and Conclusion

The rich and valuable culture of the Muh-he-ca-ne-ok, The People of the Waters That Are Never Still *will* live on.

Acknowledgements

First, my sincere thanks to Dr. Michael A. G. Haykin, FRHistS, Chair and Professor of Church History & Director of The Andrew Fuller Center for Baptist Studies at The Southern Baptist Theological Seminary, Louisville, Kentucky, for first instilling in me a love for church history and subsequently for directing and mentoring me throughout my program.

Secondly, I would like to express my appreciation to Dr. Don Lyles, my advisor at Golden State School of Theology for his guidance and direction.

Next, my unspeakable gratitude to Mr. Rick Wilcox, life-long resident of Stockbridge, Massachusetts, for tirelessly answering my correspondences and supplying me with vital supporting documentation and historical records. Thanks to Dr. Kenneth Minkema, executive director of the Jonathan Edwards Center and assistant adjunct professor of American Religious History at Yale Divinity School for providing the transcripts of Edwards' sermons.

My grateful thanks also to Mark Shaw and Heather Bruegl, as well as Yvette Malone and Larry Madden of the Arvid E. Miller Memorial Museum and Archives on the Stockbridge-Munsee Mohican Reservation in Bowler, Wisconsin.

Special thanks to Jenny Griffin, Librarian at Heritage Theological Seminary for her assistance in obtaining the books and articles I required. My gratitude also to Amelia Beaulieu for her keen eye in proofreading.

Lastly, and most importantly, I must acknowledge my dear wife, Margaret. It was she who, after I retired, recognized in me a restlessness and suggested I take "a few Bible courses." I am forever indebted to her for her constant love, consistent support and endless reading of my many papers, and helping me to achieve my goals.

About the Author

Roy M. Paul was born in Perth, Ontario. He completed a B.A. in Chemistry and Psychology from Queen's University, and an Honours B.Sc. in Biomedical Science from the University of Guelph. After a successful 25-year career as a drug product development scientist for Johnson & Johnson, he took an early retirement. Feeling unsettled and still eager to learn, Paul attended Heritage Theological Seminary in Cambridge, completing a Master of Theological Studies, magna cum laude. He subsequently went on to do a Th.D. in Church History, and currently serves as the Executive Research Assistant at the Canadian office of The Andrew Fuller Centre for Baptist Studies.

Bibliography

A Brief History of the Mohican Nation Stockbridge-Munsee Band. Bowler, WI:. Stockbridge-Munsee Historical Committee, 2017.

Berry, W. Grinton, M.A. *Foxe's Book of Martyrs*. London: The Religious Tract Society, n.d.

Brainerd, David. *Diary and Journal of David Brainerd, Volume 1*. London: Andrew Melrose, 1902.

Brewster, Paul. *Andrew Fuller: Model Pastor-Theologian*. Nashville, Tenn.: B&H Academic, 2010.

Calhoun, David B. "David Brainerd: A Constant Stream," *Presbyterion*, 13 no 1 Spr. 1987.

Carse, James. *Jonathan Edwards & The Visibility of God*, New York: Charles Scribner's Sons, 1967.

Claghorn, George S., ed. *The Works of Jonathan Edwards*. Vol. 16. New Haven: Yale University Press, 1992.

Colton, Calvin. *Tour of the American Lakes, and Among the Indians of the North-West Territory, in 1830: Disclosing the Character and Prospects of the Indian Race*. Port Washington, NY: Kennikat Press, 1972.

Cooper, James Fenimore. *The Last of the Mohicans: A Narrative of 1757*. Philadelphia: H. C. Carey & I. Lea, 1826.

Crocco, Stephen D. "Edwards's Intellectual Legacy", *The Cambridge Companion to Jonathan Edwards*, Stephen J. Stein, ed. Cambridge: Cambridge University Press, 2007.

Dallimore, Arnold A. *George Whitefield: The Life and Times of the Great Evangelist of the Eighteenth Century Revival*. Westchester, Il: Cornerstone Books, 1980.

Davidson, J. N., A.M. *Muh-He-Ka-Ne-Ok: A History of the Stockbridge Nation*. Milwaukee, WI: Silas Chapman, 1893.

DeWitt, John. Jonathan Edwards: A Study. *The Princeton Theological Review*, 1904.

Dickens, Charles and Rackman, Arthur (Illustrator). *A Christmas Carol*. New York: Weathervane Books, 1977.

Dunn, Shirley W. *The Mohican World:1680–1750*. Fleischmanns, NY: Purple Mountain Press, Ltd., 2000.

Dunn, Shirley W. *The River Indians: Mohicans Making History*. Fleischmanns, NY: Purple Mountain Press, Ltd., 2009.

Edwards, Jonathan. *A Faithful Narrative of the Surprising Work of God*. http://www.jonathan-edwards.org/Narrative.html (accessed February 13, 2018).

Edwards, Jonathan. *An Account of the Life of the late Reverend Mr. David Brainerd.* Edinburgh: John Gray and Gayin Alston, 1765.

Edwards, Jonathan. *An Humble Attempt to promote explicit agreement and visible union of God's people in extraordinary prayer for the revival of religion and the advancement of Christ's Kingdom on earth, pursuant to Scripture-promises and prophecies concerning the last time.* Boston, New England: Printed for D. Henchman in Cornhil, 1747.

Edwards, Jonathan. *The Resolutions of Jonathan Edwards*, 2006, https://www.desiringgod.org/articles/the-resolutions-of-jonathan-edwards (accessed February 13, 2018).

Edwards, Jonathan Jr., *Observations on the Language of the Muhhekaneew Indians.* New Haven: Josiah Meigs, 1788.

Faust, Clarence H. and Johnson Thomas H., eds. *Jonathan Edwards: Representative selections.* New York: American Book Company, 2002. http://mith.umd.edu/eada/html/display.php?docs=edwards_personalnarrat ive.xml&action=show.

Field, David Dudley. *Historical Sketch of the Congregational Church, Stockbridge.* Stockbridge, Berkshire County, Mass., 1888.

Frazier, Patrick. *The Mohicans of Stockbridge.* Lincoln: University of Nebraska Press, 1992.

George Whitefield's Journals. London: The Banner of Truth Trust, 1960.

Gibson, Jonathan. "Jonathan Edwards: A Missionary?" http://themelios.thegospelcoalition.org/article/jonathan-edwards-a-missionary (accessed March 20, 2019).

Goen, C.C., ed. *The Works of Jonathan Edwards.* Vol. 4. New Haven: Yale University Press, 1972.

"Gospel ministers must be fit for the Master's use, and prepared to every good work, if they would be vessels unto honour: illustrated in a sermon preached at Deerfield, August 31. 1735. At the ordination of Mr. John Sargent, to the evangelical ministry, with a special reference to the Indians of Houssatonnoc, who have lately manifested their desires to receive the Gospel." Boston: S. Kneeland & T. Green, 1735.

Hall, D., ed., *The Works of Jonathan Edwards.* Vol. 12. New Haven: Yale University Press, 1994.

Harrod, Joseph C. "A Heart Uncommonly Devoted to GOD": Theology and Piety in Jonathan Edwards' Funeral Sermon for His Daughter Jerusha, *Eusebia.* Lexington, KY: Andrew Fuller Centre for Baptist Studies, Issue 10, Fall 2008.

Hart, D. G., Sean Michael Lucas, and Stephen J. Nichols, eds. *The Legacy of Jonathan Edwards: American Religion and the Evangelical Tradition.* Grand Rapids, MI: Baker Academic, 2003.

Hatch, Nathan O., and Harry S. Stout, eds. *Jonathan Edwards And The American Dream.* Oxford: Oxford University Press, 1988.

Haykin, Michael A .G. *A Sweet Flame: Piety in the Letters of Jonathan Edwards.* Grand Rapids: Reformation Heritage Books, 2007.

Haykin, Michael A. G. *Jonathan Edwards The Holy Spirit In Revival.* Darlington, England: Evangelical Press, 2005.

Haykin, Michael A. G. *The Armies of the Lamb: The Spirituality of Andrew Fuller.* Dundas, ON: Joshua Press, 2001.

Hickman, Edward. "The True Excellency of a Gospel Minister" *The Works of Jonathan Edwards,* vol.2, revised and corr. 1834 ed., repr. Edinburgh: Banner of Truth Trust, 1974.

Hopkins, Samuel, *Historical Memoirs, Relating to the Housatunnuk Indians,* Boston: S. Kneeland, 1753.

Hopkins, Samuel. *Memoirs of the Life, Experience and Character of the Late Rev. Jonathan Edwards, A.M.* in *The Works of President Edwards* 1817 London ed.; repr. New York: Burt Franklin, 1968.

https://www.govinfo.gov/content/pkg/GPO-CONAN-1992/pdf/GPO-CONAN-1992-10-2.pdf (accessed August 20, 2019).

Hultkrantz, Ake. *The Religions of the American Indians.* Trans. by Monica Setterwall, Berkeley: University of California Press, 1979.

James, Digby L. "The Life of George Whitefield." https://banneroftruth.org/us/resources/articles/2015/life-george-whitefield/ (accessed February 17, 2018).

"Jonathan Edwards' Last Will, And The Inventory Of His Estate." *Bibliotheca Sacra.* BSAC 033:131, (Jul 1876). http://www.galaxie.com/article/bsac033-131-03 (accessed July 10, 2019).

Johnson, Thomas H. "Jonathan Edwards and the "Young Folks' Bible."" *The New England Quarterly.* 5, no.1 (Jan., 1932). https://www.jstor.org/stable/359489?read-now=1&refreqid=excelsior%3Aeb85a5623ac10ba48cf820074d6dd6be&seq=12#page_scan_tab_contents (accessed June 26, 2019).

Jones, Electa F. *Stockbridge Past and Present or, Records of an Old Mission Station.* Springfield, Mass.: Samuel Bowles & Company, 1854.

Journal of the Evangelical Theological Society. La Mirada, CA, Volume 62, No. 3, September, 2019.

Kidwell, Clara Sue, Homer Noley, and George E. "Tink" Tinker. *A Native American Theology.* Maryknoll, NY: Orbis Books, 2001.

Kimnach, Wilson H., ed. *The Works of Jonathan Edwards.* Vol. 25. New Haven:
    Yale University Press, 2006.

Kimnach, Wilson H., Kenneth P. Minkema, and Douglas A. Sweeney, eds.
    The Sermons of Jonathan Edwards. New Haven: Yale University Press, 1999.

Lesser, M.X. *Jonathan Edwards*. Boston, Mass.: Twayne Publishers, 1988.
Liardon, Roberts. "George Whitefield," God's Generals, 2018. http://godsgenerals.com/georgewhitefiele/ (accessed February 18).
Love, W. DeLoss. *Samson Occom and the Christian Indians of New England*. Boston: The Pilgrim's Press, 1899.
Lutheran Church of the Wilderness. https://www.lutheranchurchofthewilderness.com/history (accessed September 4, 2019).
Marsden, George M. *A Short Life of Jonathan Edwards*. Grand Rapids: William B. Eerdmans Publishing Company, 2008.
Marsden, George M. *Jonathan Edwards: A Life*. New Haven: Yale University Press, 2003.
McClymond, Michael J. and Gerald R. McDermott. *The Theology of Jonathan Edwards*. Oxford: Oxford University Press, 2012.
McDermott, Gerald R. *Jonathan Edwards Confronts the Gods: Christian Theology, Enlightenment Religion, and Non-Christian Faiths*. Oxford: Oxford University Press, 2000.
McDermott, Gerald R. *Understanding Jonathan Edwards*. Oxford: Oxford University Press, 2009.
Miles, Lion G. *A Life of John Konkapot: The Mohican Chief Who Sold His Berkshire Hunting Grounds to Puritan Settlers, Hoping That Their Faith and Example Would Benefit His People*. New Marlborough, MA: Historical Society of New Marlborough, 2009.
Miles, Lion G. "The Red Man Dispossessed: The Williams Family and the Alienation of Indian Land in Stockbridge, Massachusetts, 1736-1818." *The New England Quarterly* 68, 1994.
Murray, Iain H. *Jonathan Edwards-A New Biography*. Edinburgh: The Banner of Truth Trust, 1987.
Nettles, Thomas J. "The Influence of Jonathan Edwards on Andrew Fuller," E*usebia*, 9 (2008): 97-116.
Nichols, Stephen J. *Jonathan Edwards: A Guided Tour of His Life and Thought*. Phillipsburg: P&R Publishing, 2001.
Oberle, James. *A Nation of Statesmen: The Political Culture of the Stockbridge-Munsee Mohicans, 1815-1972*. Norman: University of Oklahoma Press, 2005.
Ortlund, Dane C. *Edwards on the Christian Life: Alive to the Beauty of God*. Wheaton, Illinois: Crossway, 2014.
Pettit, Norman, ed. *The Works of Jonathan Edwards*. Vol. 7. New Haven: Yale University Press, 1985.
Peyer, Bernd C., ed. *American Indian Nonfiction: An Anthology of Writings, 1760s-1930s*. Norman: University of Oklahoma Press, 2007.
Piper, John. *God's Passion for his Glory: Living the Vision of Jonathan Edwards*. Wheaton, IL: Crossway, 2006.

Putnam, Thelma. *Christian Religion Among the Stockbridge Munsee Band of Mohican Indians.* Arvid E. Miller Memorial Museum and Archives, Bowler, WI. n.d.

Ramerini, Marco. "Dutch New York: The Dutch settlements in North America." https://www.colonialvoyage.com/dutch-new-york/ (accessed July 25, 2019).

Rutherford, Adam. "A New History of the First Peoples in the Americas." *The Atlantic.* 2017. https://www.theatlantic.com/science/archive/2017/10/a-brief-history-of-everyone-who-ever-lived/537942/ (accessed July 23, 2019).

Ryland, John. The Indwelling and Righteousness of Christ no Security against Corporeal Death, but the Source of Spiritual and Eternal Life. London: W. Button & Sons, 1815.

Sedgwick, Sarah Cabot and Christina Sedgwick Marquand. *Stockbridge 1739-1939: A Chronicle.* Great Barrington, MA.: The Berkshire Courier, 1939.

Shaw, Mark, ed. *Reflections on the Waters That Are Never Still: A Literary Journal of the Mohican People.* Saline, MI: McNaughton & Gunn, 2015.

Shelton, Don O. *David Brainerd: Chronology of Life*, https://www.wholesomewords.org/missions/biobrainerd5.html (accessed March 5, 2018).

Siemers, Jeffrey. *Proud and Determined: A History of the Stockbridge Mohicans, 1734-2014.* Fond du Lac, Wisconsin: Big Smokey Press, 2013.

Silverman, David J. Red Brethren: *The Brothertown and Stockbridge Indians and the Problem of Race in Early America.* NY: Cornell University Press, 2010.

Smith, J.E.A. *History of Pittsfield, (Berkshire County), Massachusetts, From the year 1734 to the year 1800.* Boston: Lee and Shephard, 1869.

Smith, Oswald J. *David Brainerd: Man of Prayer.* London: Marshall, Morgan and Scott, 1975.

Stein, Stephen J., ed. *The Cambridge Companion To Jonathan Edwards.* Cambridge: Cambridge University Press, 2007.

Stoddard, Solomon. *Question whether God is not Angry with the Country for doing so little towards the Conversion of the Indians?* https://quod.lib.umich.edu/cgi/t/text/text-idx?c=evans;cc=evans;view=text;idno=N02091.0001.001;rgn=div1;node=N02091.0001.001:1 (accessed June 25, 2019).

"Stories of the Lenape People with translations in the Lenape Language" as told by Chief Robert Red Hawk Ruth, Lenape Nation of Pennsylvania. Library at Delaware Nation of Moraviantown, Thamesville, Ontario.

Stout, Harry S. "Edwards and Revival." In *Understanding Jonathan Edwards.* ed. Gerald R. McDermott, Oxford: Oxford University Press, 2009.

Stout, Harry S., and Nathan O. Hatch, eds. The Works of Jonathan Edwards. Vol. 22. New Haven: Yale University Press, 2003.

Strachan, Owen and Doug Sweeney. *Jonathan Edwards, Lover of God.* Chicago,

Il.: Moody Publishers, 2010.

The Assembly's Shorter Catechism. Arvid E. Miller Memorial Museum and Archives, Bowler, WI.

The Lutheran Church Missouri Synod. http://locator.lcms.org/nchurches_frm/c_graphs.asp?C382025 (accessed September 4, 2019).

The Select Works of Jonathan Edwards, Vol. II. London: Banner of Truth Trust, 1959.

The Westminster Shorter Catechism. https://bpc.org/wp-content/uploads/2015/06/d-scatechism.pdf (accessed July 26, 2019).

Walling, Richard S. *Death in the Bronx: The Stockbridge Indian Massacre, August 1778.* Hudson, NY: Native American Institute at Columbia-Greene Community College, 1999.

Wheeler, Rachel. *To Live Upon Hope.* Ithaca, New York: Cornell University Press, 2008.

Wheeler, Rachel. "Hendrick Aupaumut: Christian-Mahican Prophet." *Journal of the Early Republic.* 25, No.2 (Summer, 2005): 187–220.

Wright, Harry Andrews, ed. *Indian Deeds of Hampden County.* Springfield MA: 1905.

Wright, Wyllis E. *Colonel Ephraim Williams: A Documentary Life.* Pittsfield, Mass.: Berkshire County Historical Society, 1970.

Winslow, Ola Elizabeth. *Jonathan Edwards, 1703–1758: A Biography.* New York: McMillan Co., 1940.

Zotigh, Dennis. "Native Perspectives on the 40th Anniversary of The American Indian Religious Freedom Act." https://www.smithsonianmag.com/blogs/national-museum-american-indian/2018/11/30/native-perspectives-american-indian-religious-freedom-act/ (accessed August 19, 2019).

Subject Index

A

American Indian Religious Freedom Act, 49
Appleton, Nathaniel, 23
Aristotle, 79
Arminianism, 85
Ashley, John, 11, 20, 95
Ashley, Jonathan, 91
Aupaumut, Hendrick, 1, 4, 5, 6, 7, 37, 38, 41, 46, 47
Ayscough, Francis, 55, 56, 60

B

Baker, Noah, 79
Baptism, 18, 22, 24, 28, 35, 51, 52, 71, 83, 123, 127, 130, 132, 133, 138
Baskett, John, 55
Bathsheba, 79, 80
Belcher, Jonathan, 10, 12, 14, 15, 23
Brainerd, David, xvi, 88
Brown, Samuel, 30, 152
Bull, Nehemiah, 15, 16, 17, 18, 21
Burns, David, 79
Burr Jr., Aaron, 101
Burr Sr., Aaron, 101, 161
Burr, Esther. *See* Edwards, Esther
Burt, Elkanah, 79
Burts, Samuell, 79

C

Canada, 9, 87, 132, 135, 152
Carter, Jimmy, 49
Caughnawaga Tribe, 23
Chanequin, James, 94, 95
Chauncy, Charles, 75
Choate, Joseph Hodges, 59
Choate, Mabel, 59, 60
Clark, Joanna, 80
Colman, Benjamin, 13, 22, 27, 72, 73
Colton, Calvin, 57
Coram, Thomas, 55, 56

D

Davenport, James, 75
Davids, James, 61
Declaration of Independence, 101
Deism, 87
Delaware Tribe, 37
Dickens, Charles, 115
Diseases, 4, 7, 29
Doxtator, Ethel, 52
Dwight, Henry, 11, 99
Dwight, Sereno E., 63

E

East India Company, 2
Edwards, Esther, 101, 102, 153
Edwards, Esther Stoddard, 64
Edwards, Hannah, 27
Edwards, Jonathan
   70 Resolutions, 103, 104, 105
   assumes pulpit in Stockbridge, 34, 123
   birth, 64
   call to Stockbridge, 86
   Calvinism, 90, 156
   children, 74, 101, 123, 153, 172
   church covenant, 81

death, 63, 101, 102, 162
dismissal from Northampton, 77
education, 65
family, 27, 74, 81, 85, 87, 94
final words, 102
half-way covenant, 71, 82, 169
illness, 72, 152, 172
leaves Stockbridge, 101
marriage, 70, 75, 101
Mohican language, 94, 123
on prayer, 105, 106, 107, 166
on the Lord's Supper, 71, 77, 82
opposition, 75, 82, 83, 85, 152, 170
president of College of New Jersey (Princeton), 34, 101, 162
revival, 72, 73, 74, 76, 105, 106, 108
salary, 70, 77, 84
Sinners in the Hands of an Angry God, 107, 121, 133, 149
suicide of his uncle, Joseph Hawley, 73
Young Folks Bible, 79
Edwards, Jonathan Jr., xv, 94, 123, 172
Edwards, Lucy, 101
Edwards, Sarah, 69, 84, 101, 102
Edwards, Timothy, 64, 65, 67, 71
Emigrant Party, 38
Erskine, John, 87
Etowaukaum, 12, 20
Etowwohkaum, Jonas, 94, 95
Excommunication, 31, 35

F

Franklin, Benjamin, 104
Frederick (Prince of Wales), 55
French and Indian war, 153
French and Indian War, 34, 87

G

Garrick, David, 108
Genocide, 3, 38
Goltz, Rolland, 52
Grant, William, 13
Great Awakening, 74
Great Land Grab, 93

H

Hall, David, 85
Hamilton, Alexander, 101
Hannam, Eleazar, 77
Hannam, Moses, 80
Hawley, Joseph, 73
Hendrick, Lydia, 38
Hitchcock, Luke, 11
Hollis, Isaac, 96, 97, 98, 99, 100
Hooker, Thomas, 68
Hopkins, Electa, 28
Hopkins, Mark, 28, 96
Hopkins, Samuel, xv, 3, 13, 14, 15, 33, 78
Hubbard, Thomas, 97
Hudson, Henry, 2, 3, 174

I

Immanuel Mohican Indian Lutheran Church, 51, 52
Indian Removal Act, 38, 173
Ingersole, Thomas, 25, 26
Iroquois Tribe, 135

J

Jackson, Andrew, 38
James, Elizabeth. *See* Whitefield, Elizabeth
Jefferson, Thomas, 101

Jenks, Betty, 79
John Samuel Hopkins. *See* Konkapot, John
Jones, Electa, 2
Jones, Josiah, 30, 95

K

Kellogg, Joseph, 23, 96
Kellogg, Martin, 97, 98, 152
Konkapot, John, 6, 12, 14, 15, 19, 20, 21, 22, 24, 26, 29, 30, 45, 96
Konkapot, Mary, 29
Kunkapot, 20, 22, 24, 29
Kunkapot, Mary, 24

L

Lancton, John, 79
Last of the Mohicans, xvii
Latimer, Hugh, 160
Lutheran Church of the Wilderness, 51

M

Marquand, Christina Sedgwick, 91, 153
Massacre of 1704, 23
McCullough, William, 76
Menominee Tribe, 38
Merrick, Joseph, 46
Metoxen, 20
Miami Tribe, 37
Mission House, 27, 28, 59, 60
Mohawk Tribe, 10, 18, 91, 96, 97, 98, 99, 135, 170
Mohegan Tribe, xvii, 37
Mohican Tribe
  alcohol, 4, 5, 10, 11, 19, 21, 22, 24, 30, 33, 165, 166

catechism, 41, 47
church split, 37
Citizen Party, 38
debt, 6, 35
farming, 6, 25, 91
first convert, 18
founding of Stockbridge, 26
Great, Good Spirit, xvii, 41, 42, 43, 45, 46, 49
hunting, 5, 6, 133
Indian Party, 38
infant mortality, 29
land, 11, 31, 34, 37, 48, 93, 173
marriage, 43, 44
massacre, 152, 161
origin, 1
racism, 31
rebel group, 38
school, 99
schools, xviii, 22, 28, 30, 35, 52, 55, 92, 97, 152
Stockbridge Bible, 51, 52, 55, 57, 58, 60, 61
Monotheism, 41
Moravian Missionaries, 33
Mtohksin
  see Metoxen, 20
Munsee Tribe, 3, 2, 38, 39, 177

N

New Netherlands Company of Amsterdam., 3
New Stockbridge, 28, 37, 47, 93
Nungkawwat, 20

O

Occom, Samson, 37
Old Stockbridge Orthodox Presbyterian Church, 51, 52

Oneida Tribe, 37
Our Saviour's Lutheran Church, 50, 51, 52

P

Paice, Joseph, 97
Pepperell, William, 97
Peqout Tribe, xvii
Pierpont, James, 68
Pomeroy, Ebenezer, 25, 26
Pomeroy, Seth, 79, 80
Poohpoonuc, Ebenezer, 16, 18, 21, 24, 123
Poohpoonuc, Sarah, 24
Price, Hiram, 48
Prince, Thomas, 74, 81, 99, 120
Princeton University, xviii, 101, 161

Q

Queen Anne's War, 9
Quinney, Jamieson "Sote", 58
Quinney, Joseph, 47

R

Religious Freedom, 48, 49, 173
Revolutionary War, 35
Ridley, Nicholas, 160
Rinehard, Roy, 52
Roman Catholicism, 4, 13, 18, 132
Root, Simeon, 80
Root, Timothy, 79, 80

S

Sarah Pierpont. *See* Edwards, Sarah
Sargeant, John, 28
Schaghticoke Tribe, 23
Scotland, 85, 87

Scrooge, Ebenezer, 115
Sedgwick, Sarah Cabot, 91, 153
Sergeant Jr., John, 28, 35, 37, 38
Sergeant Memorial Church, 50, 58, 60
Sergeant, Abigail, 27, 28, 33, 34, 86
Sergeant, Electa, 2
  see Hopkins, Electa, 28
Sergeant, Erastus, 28
Sergeant, John, xviii, 17, 18, 19, 21, 22, 23, 26, 27, 29, 31, 32, 45, 50, 55, 56, 58, 59, 60, 86, 91, 93, 95, 97, 123, 131, 169, 170, 172
Seven Years' War, 158
Shepard, Gordon, 53
Sherman, Thomas, 95
Shute, John, 55
Slingerland, Jeremiah, 58
Sonkenewenaukheek.
  See Umpachenee, Aaron
Stiles, Ezra, 63, 86, 87
Stiles, Isaac, 87
Stockbridge Bible Church, 51, 52
Stoddard, John, 9, 10, 11, 13, 20, 25, 26, 70, 169
Stoddard, Solomon, 8, 9, 10, 65, 68, 70, 71, 72, 77, 83, 84, 141, 169

T

Teller, I. M., 48
Tobacco, 5, 51
Treaty of Westminster, 3

U

Umpachenee, Aaron, 6, 12, 15, 18, 19, 20, 21, 24, 25, 29, 30, 31, 33, 34, 96
Umpachenee, Hannah, 29

V

Van Slingerlandt, Teunis Cornelise, 92
VanGilder, John, 11

W

Warner, Oliver, 80
Washington, George, 37
Waters, Moll, 79
Wauwaumpequuanaunt, John, 124
Wesley, Charles, 74
Wesley, John, 74
West, Stephen, 34, 35, 46
Westfall, Frederick G., 58, 59, 60
Whitefield, George, 74, 75, 108, 120
Widows, 45, 86

Williams Jr., Ephraim, 91
Williams, Abigail, 91
   see Sergeant, Abigail, 27
Williams, Elisha, 84
Williams, Ephraim, 27, 30, 34, 86, 91, 93, 97, 98, 152
Williams, Israel, 82
Williams, John, 9, 14
Williams, Solomon, 83, 84
Williams, Stephen, 14, 15, 16, 18, 20, 23, 24, 33, 119
Williams, William, 23
Winnebago Tribe, 38
W-naum-pee, 22
Woodbridge, Joseph, 30
Woodbridge, Timothy, 18, 20, 22, 26, 27, 95, 98, 100
World War I, 50

Scripture Index

Genesis
- 4:9 169

Exodus
- 20:12 44
- 20:16 44
- 20:1–17 44

Leviticus
- 19:18 44
- 19:36 44

Deuteronomy
- 6:6–7 44
- 7:3–4 44
- 15:11 44
- 32:35 110

2 Chronicles
- 20:6 154

Job
- 14:5 159
- 32:11 113

Proverbs
- 6:17 44
- 6:6–12 44
- 12:17 44
- 12:24 44
- 14:5 44
- 14:23 44
- 16:11 44
- 20:6 104
- 21:5 44
- 22:9 44
- 25:21 44
- 26:27 156

Ecclesiastes
- 2:16 113
- 8:8 157

Isaiah
- 25:8 107
- 25:9 107
- 40:8 150
- 57:20 113
- 59:18 117
- 63:3 118
- 66:15 117

Jeremiah
- 17:9 169

Ezekiel
- 8:18 117

Zechariah
- 8:20–22 106

Matthew
- 5:9 44
- 5:42 44
- 6:30 149
- 10:28 160
- 15:4 44
- 18:19 107
- 25:35–40 44
- 28:19 8

Mark
- 7:10 44

Luke
- 12:4 117
- 12:5 117
- 18:20 44
- 21:36 165

John
- 3:18 112

Acts
- 11:12–13 .... 125, 126

Romans
- 1:20 41

5:6 110	6:6–8 104
8:26 104	**Colossians**
10:14 3	3:14 44
13:1–7 44	**2 Thessalonians**
1 Corinthians	3:10 44
12:13 161	**Hebrews**
15:54–55 160	2:14–15 161
16:14 44	9:27 159
2 Corinthians	12:14 44
4:18 .... 143, 149	12:15–16 78
5:9–10 166	13:2 44
6:14–17 44	13:6 44
13:11 44	13:8 164
Galatians	13:16 44
4:4 110	13:7–8 162
5:22 160	**1 Peter**
5:23 160	1:24–25 150
5:22–23 104	2:13–17 44
6:9 44	4:9 44
Ephesians	**Revelation**
6:2 44	19:15 117
6:12 112	

Date Read	Name

H&E Publishing

WWW.HesedAndEmet.com

www.ingramcontent.com/pod-product-compliance
Lightning Source LLC
Chambersburg PA
CBHW060355080526
44583CB00012B/320